Masterpieces of
TUTANKHAMUN

Masterpieces of

TUTANK

HAMUN

INTRODUCTION AND COMMENTARIES BY

DAVID P. SILVERMAN

ABBEVILLE PRESS • PUBLISHERS • NEW YORK

With love
to my wife Melanie

The following photographs were supplied by:

Scala/Editorial Photocolor Archives (EPA) (pages 13
through 27, 35 through 39, 47, 73, 79, 81, 91, 99 through
105, 111, 119, 125, 129, 131, 135, 145, 147, 151, 155)
Borromeo/Scala EPA (pages 39, 71, 133, 149)

Library of Congress Cataloging in Publication Data

Silverman, David P.
  Masterpieces of Tutankhamun.

  1. Tutankhamun, King of Egypt—Tomb.   2. Egypt—
Antiquities.   3. Art objects, Egyptian. I. Title.
DT87.5.S45   709'.32   78-12357

ISBN 0-89659-022-4

CONTENTS

INTRODUCTION

When Tutankhamun came to the throne, around 1334 B.C., he was barely nine years old, and Egypt was still under the effects of the religious changes introduced by his predecessor, Akhenaton. It was the fate of the young king, who ruled only a few years, to be the central figure in restoring his homeland to order. Less than fifteen years prior to his coronation, Akhenaton, whose original name was Amenhotep IV, had moved the capital of Egypt from Thebes to a virgin site about two hundred miles further north, which he called Akhetaton (modern Tell el Amarna). In translation, Akhetaton means "the horizon of the Aton," a reference to the focus of the new religion, the disk of the sun, called the Aton.

The religion that Akhenaton instituted suppressed most of the gods of the Egyptian pantheon, some of which had already been worshipped for thousands of years, and it brought new emphasis to the role of the king. In many ways there was almost an equality between Akhenaton and the Aton. Both had jubilees and cartouches (elliptically-shaped outlines encircling the written name of the king) which previously had been royal prerogatives. The king, like the former gods of Egypt, now had his own high priest; his subjects worshipped him, and he was their intermediary to the Aton. No longer were they to pray directly to the Aton. The people were to bow down to Akhenaton and his wife Nefertiti when the couple were presented on days of festival. Previously, the gods in their sacred barks would be brought to the people during such holidays.

This iconoclastic trend entered other aspects of Egyptian culture as well. The classical language was altered to reflect more of the spoken language, and Egyptian art, which had maintained a consistent style and iconography for almost two thousand years, became more expressionistic and experimental.

Many people have seen the origins of monotheism in Akhenaton's movement, since there was an emphasis upon one god. The king took pains to have the plural signs obliterated from the word 'gods' and to erase the names of other deities. However, he himself was treated as a god. Not all gods were abandoned, and the goddess Maat, who represented balance and harmony, often appears as a gift to the Aton from the king so as to illustrate the order brought about by his reign. There is evidence from Akhetaton that some people still retained images of their old gods, despite their acceptance of the new theology. Toward the end of Akhenaton's reign it appears that a return to Thebes and to the traditional beliefs was imminent.

The death of Akhenaton, a visible inconsistency with his self-proclaimed divinity, must have contributed greatly to the people's inability to accept completely the new doctrines. His named successor, Smenkhkara, scarcely survived the death of Akhenaton. The throne then passed to a nine-year-old child, Tutankhaton, who was married to the royal princess Ankhesenpaaton. While his parentage is still unclear, it seems certain that he was directly related to the king. His claim to the throne was secured through his marriage, since his wife was the daughter of Akhenaton and Nefertiti. Their original religious affiliation is clearly indicated by their Atonist names; these, however, were altered later, and there is reason to believe that even while the royal pair ruled at Akhetaton, a strong tendency toward the old religion was growing. This period of transition represented a coexistence of the two doctrines. Some of the objects in Tutankhamun's tomb reflect elements of both Aton and Amon beliefs. The king's new name, Tutankhamun, meaning "Living image of Amon" or "Perfect is the life of Amon," was adopted in the third year of his reign. At that time he chose the traditional sites of Memphis in the north and Thebes in the south as his capitals.

In recording his deeds after he became king, he emphasized the chaotic condition in which he found the land; the country and its temples had deteriorated, and shrines and chapels had been abandoned. As described by Tutankhamun, Egypt was in such a state that prayers to gods went unanswered. But it was he who rescued the land and restored order. Such boasts, however, were traditionally made by Egyptian kings who, when they assumed the divine office of kingship, symbolically became the ruler who united the lands of Upper and Lower Egypt and turned chaos into order. It would appear that Tutankhamun's statements may have had more validity than those of some of his predecessors.

Tutankhamun had little opportunity to prove his own abilities, since he died when he was eighteen or nineteen years old. Despite his youth, it is possible that he had already begun to take a more active role as king. Considering the amount of military equipment in his tomb, he may have taken a part, even if only a minor one, in battle. Building projects were begun in his name by the time he was a teenager, and he completely decorated the colonnade at the Temple of Amon at Luxor, begun by Amenhotep III, with illustrations of the important Festival of Opet. The style of art during his reign illustrates the state of transition. The iconography tends to be traditional, while the treatment of subject matter is more reminiscent of the expressionistic style prevalent during Akhenaton's reign.

Tutankhamun hardly deserves to be called a minor king. During the ten years that he was on the throne, Egypt could boast a record of major accomplishments: a peaceful counter-reformation was established, foreign affairs were settled, and order was brought to a land that had been in the king's own words, "topsy-turvy."

Considering his return to tradition, Tutankhamun should have prepared a final resting place for himself in the Valley of the Kings, the site of the tombs of all the kings of the Eighteenth Dynasty from the time of Thutmosis I to Amenhotep III. But, since he began his rule at Akhetaton, it is likely that work on his tomb in Thebes did not begin for several years, if at all. His early death from unknown causes in 1325 B.C. would hardly have allowed for the completion of a tomb on the scale of his

predecessor's. While the seventy days necessary for the process of mummification elapsed, an alternate place of burial, still in the Valley, was prepared for him. In place, location, and decoration this tomb is unlike those of his predecessors, but it is similar in design to the tomb of the maternal grandparents of Akhenaton, who were also interred in the Valley of the Kings.

It has been suggested that Tutankhamun's tomb might originally have belonged to his aged mentor Aye, the man who eventually succeeded him. Considering the tomb's small size, absence of most decoration, and the probability of a non-royal owner, its location may not have been known to many people. In addition, the rather strict surveillance of the necropolis during the next few reigns probably contributed to the survival of Tutankhamun's tomb into modern times. It is also possible that natural phenomena, such as violent rain storms and the resulting mud and gravel slides, further obscured the entrance to the tomb. The fact that its location had been kept secret is supported by the presence of the tomb of the pharaoh, Ramesses VI, built almost directly above, two hundred years later. While carving the later tomb out of the living rock, the workers never discovered the earlier one, scarcely a few feet away. They dumped their debris over the already hidden entrance and thus inadvertently succeeded in maintaining its obscurity and saved it from the ravaging tomb robbers of the late Ramesside period. Moreover, they erected some of their huts directly over the tomb of the young king.

For three thousand more years the tomb of Tutankhamun remained hidden. Although his monuments had been appropriated by successors and his name omitted in some later king lists, his existence was attested by the few times his name appears untouched. Attempts had been made to locate his tomb, and the unimpressive finds made in 1908 in the Valley of the Kings by the American, Theodore Davis, were accepted as the meager remains of the king. The British archaeologist Howard Carter, however, believed that Tutankhamun's tomb had not yet been located and that earlier discoveries were merely clues to its location. Using the earlier finds as his boundaries, in 1915 he began to excavate the area which they outlined. Generously supported by his patron, Lord Carnarvon,

Carter painstakingly examined this area for several years without any real success. Lord Carnarvon had almost given up hope for the project, but Carter convinced him to maintain a seventh, and final season. Carter began work at the ancient huts near the entrance to the Tomb of Ramesses VI early in November, 1922, scarcely a week into the new season. After a few days the huts were properly recorded and removed, and Carter could excavate the site. The next morning, November 4, 1922, a step, cut in the rock, had been uncovered just below the entrance to the tomb of Ramesses VI. There were sixteen steps in all, beyond which lay the sealed entrance to a tomb. Work stopped for a few weeks until Lord Carnarvon, who was in England, could reach Luxor. On November 23, with the entire crew present, the work began again. By the next afternoon, the seals of Tutankhamun on the plastered doorway to the entrance corridor were positively identified. In addition, Carter discovered secondary plaster sealing, evidence that the tomb had been resealed twice. It was later discerned that the intrusions occurred within a few years after Tutankhamun's burial.

Having broken down the sealed doorway, Carter began to clear the entrance corridor, which descended about thirty feet into the bedrock. He noted the presence of a robber's tunnel and discovered some leather water skins, which he later deduced had been used in the second robbery attempt when the precious oils and unguents were stolen. The thieves, aware of the difficulty and impracticality of transporting the heavy alabaster jars, came prepared with skins into which they could pour the oil. The first intrusion, Carter was to learn, was made to steal the objects of precious metal.

On November 26, with the corridor cleared, the excavators stood before another sealed doorway. This one led to the first of four rooms, which were literally filled with burial equipment for the young king. Carter, however, was unaware of what lay before him when he poked a hole in the upper left-hand corner and inserted a rod. He felt no resistance. After first testing for noxious fumes, he finally felt secure enough to enlarge the opening so he could peer in. Carter's amazement at the sight prevented him from speaking until Lord Carnarvon, standing impatiently nearby, brought him back to reality by asking what could be seen.

This room was the Antechamber, the first of the four in the tomb and the only one that Lord Carnarvon would live to see examined completely. Carter's team continued to work in the tomb, recording, photographing, and conserving. Almost ten years passed before all the material was safely housed in the Cairo Museum. The mummy, however, replaced in its outer coffin, still remains in the original sarcophagus in the Burial Chamber of the tomb.

The tomb of Tutankhamun is the only royal burial in the Valley of the Kings that was found almost completely intact. But, despite the wealth of material, approximately 5,000 inventoried pieces, Carter estimated that almost eighty percent of the jewelry and objects of precious metal had been stolen in the first robbery attempt. Still, what remained in the tomb provided the world with the most exciting archaeological discovery of all time. The contents of the tomb provide much general information about Egypt in the latter part of the Eighteenth Dynasty, but still they leave unanswered many questions regarding the life of the king, his family, and the fate of his widow.

By discovering the tomb and its contents, Carter was able to grant the young king a form of immortality. Now, Tutankhamun has indeed been "given life forever," the phrase which so often accompanies his representations.

Statue of Amenhotep III
Being Conducted by the God Amon

THE HEADLESS LIMESTONE FIGURE of the god Amon stands behind the pharaoh Amenhotep III and brings him forward. Amon was the national god of Egypt during the New Kingdom and as such had vast endowments and estates assigned to him; his priesthood, therefore, was both powerful and wealthy. The closeness of the royal family with this god can be seen by the name Amenhotep, which many of the Eighteenth Dynasty kings had. It means "Amon is peaceful/satisfied." While it is clear that Tutankhamun's roots also can be traced to this family, it is not certain whether Amenhotep III was his father or grandfather. Much of the material surviving from Tutankhamun's time reflects the return to the traditional gods of ancient Egypt and an attempt to negate the era of the preceding Amarna controversy. It is likely, therefore, that Tutankhamun would have omitted any reference to that period and would have wished to stress his continuity with the ancient traditions of Egypt. The fact that he refers to Amenhotep III as his father despite the fact that he may have been his grandfather, perhaps relates to this tendency. Although Tutankhamun reaffirmed the traditions of the past and denied links to the Amarna period, traces of that period are evident in both art and inscriptions.

Decoration from the Palace of Amenhotep III at Malkata

AMENHOTEP III BUILT AN ELABORATE PALACE on the West Bank, across the river and southwest of the city of Thebes. It is situated south of his funerary temple in front of which were the colossi of Memnon. The palace grounds covered an area of over eighty acres and consisted of several family estates, both large and small, villas for a few high officials, smaller residences for others, and a workmen's village, in addition to the residence of the king and his wife Queen Tiye. The vast gardens that complemented the site are reflected in this fragment of a wall of the palace. Stylized rosettes between horizontal bands border the top of the marsh scene. A large clump of papyrus is on the left, while a bird appears to be alighting in the vegetation on the right. Such scenes, part of the repertoire of Egyptian artists, appear on the walls of contemporary as well as earlier tombs. The action is much more static, and the vegetation is rendered in stiffer and more angular lines.

Similar representations occur as decoration at the site of Akhenaton's capital Akhetaton (modern Tell el Amarna) on both the walls and floors of the estates. The influence for this decoration at Amarna is clearly that of Malkata, for Akhenaton and his wife spent many years at Malkata and had a residence there during the reign of Amenhotep III. Similar motifs can be found on objects from the tomb of Tutankhamun; the golden shrine (page 55), not visible in this view, and the elaborately decorated chest (page 35), but they follow the more traditional and less lively style of the past.

Several theories have been proposed regarding Tutankhamun's genealogy. Some scholars have suggested that Tutankhamun was born at Malkata, as the last child of Amenhotep III and Queen Tiye, while others feel that he was born most likely at Akhetaton, probably to Akhenaton and a minor wife. It is not known for certain whether Tutankhamun chose Malkata as his own residence upon his return to Thebes.

14

Chair of Sitamun,
Daughter of Amenhotep III

SITAMUN, WHOSE NAME MEANS "DAUGHTER OF AMON," was the eldest daughter of Amenhotep III and Queen Tiye. She, along with the other members of her family, lived at the large palace complex of her father at Malkata, where her own extensive estate was situated in the northern part of the site. While her importance during the reign of Amenhotep III and his successor, Akhenaton, was evidently considerable, judging from the surviving information, there is no indication of whether she was the mother of either Smenkhkare or Tutankhamun. Her own burial place was in a separate part of the tomb of Amenhotep III.

This chair of reddish wood covered with both silver and gold, however, was not part of Sitamun's burial equipment, but an apparent gift for her maternal grandparents Yuya and Thuya, since it was found in their small tomb in the Valley of the Kings. Its shape is similar to that of the throne chair found in the tomb of Tutankhamun. The legs take the shape of feline paws, and each rests on a low silver-covered support, which may have been a protective element designed to raise the elaborately carved details of the legs up and away from possible damage. Protruding from the front of the seat on each side is the bust of a woman, all features of which, except the wig, are gilded. Lions' heads were the typical decoration here in most other royal chairs of the New Kingdom. The frame of the seat, which, like the back, shows indications of being veneered, supports a woven seat. The raised relief on the back is gilded as well and portrays the seated princess twice. Before each representation of her is a woman presenting a necklace, and the scene extends to the inner panels of the arms where female offerers present golden rings. On one side of the outer panels the goddess Taweret is flanked by two representations of the god Bes, and on the other there are three of Bes alone. The hieroglyphs on the back identify the princess and label the accompanying offering scene as "presenting the gold of the southern foreign lands." Three vertical posts support the slanted back. The elaborately carved and gilded wings on the top of the back are paralleled in the wooden chair from the tomb of Tutankhamun.

16

Upper Portion of a Statue
of Amenhotep IV

ORIGINALLY THIS FRAGMENT of a colossal limestone statue was one of
several that stood in the Temple to the Aton which Amenhotep IV
built to the east of the Temple of Amon at Karnak. The carefully
exaggerated features of the king's physiognomy are typical of the
earlier part of his reign. While it is clear that the traditional style of
Egyptian art has been abandoned here in favor of a more
expressionistic one, the attitude and placement of the statue follows
the patterns already in use for over one thousand years. Like other
pharaohs before him, Akhenaton wears the *nemes* headdress—
a striped headcloth with projecting uraeus (serpent), a royal crown,
a false beard, and he carries the crook and the flail in his crossed
arms. Other more complete examples indicate that the statues were
not in the form of the god Osiris, however, since they wore kilts
rather than the traditional mummy wrappings. On his wrist is a
bracelet with two cartouches (elliptical outlines enclosing a
hieroglyphic inscription designating the name of a king or queen). It
is not his name that is depicted, but that of the Aton, the disk of the
sun which formed the basis of his new religion. These designations
serve to identify the king with his new god.

The temple and the statues must have been constructed around
the fifth or sixth year of his reign, just prior to the changing of his
name from Amenhotep IV to Akhenaton and his moving the capital
from Thebes in the south to Akhetaton in Middle Egypt. With the
development of the new religion, which emphasized the visible
manifestation of the sun, its disk (the Aton), came a new style of art,
tending more toward realism than was typical before. While more
exaggerated at first, as is evidenced by this statue, the style became,
in most cases, more realistic after the move to Amarna, as can be
seen by the famous bust of Nefertiti in the Berlin Museum. Judging
from the physical remains of members of the family, an elongated
skull and a broad jaw may have been a familial characteristic, but
the statue still must be understood as an artist's interpretation rather
than as an accurate representation. Although it is possible that
Akhenaton was the father of Tutankhamun, some scholars have
suggested that he was his brother.

Painted Stela with Akhenaton, Nefertiti, and Three Daughters

CARVED IN SUNK RELIEF, this limestone stela depicts Akhenaton, his wife Nefertiti, and three of their daughters. Meryetaton, the eldest, stands between her parents, Meketaton stands on her mother's lap, and Ankhesenpaaton, the future wife of Tutankhamun, is seated on Nefertiti's lap. The long, dark, horizontal carving at the top of the scene is the hieroglyph *pet* ("sky") under which is the Aton, the disk of the sun, which has a uraeus (serpent) at the base with the hieroglyph *ankh* ("life") around its neck. The rays of the sun fan out over the entire family, and each ray ends in a hand. Those rays near the head of the king and queen extend *ankhs* toward the noses of the royal couple. The outer border contains an inscription which records the names and designations of the Aton and the royal family. The architectonic design of this limestone stela is enhanced by the elaborate top, called a cavetto cornice, and the post holes for doors are carved in the base.

This stela was meant to be a household shrine, and it was found near one of the houses at Akhetaton. The intimacy of the scene marks a departure from traditional iconography which rarely shows depictions of the private lives of royal families. The style, while less exaggerated, is not totally naturalistic, and the use of the name of the Aton, introduced in the eighth year of the reign would justify dating the piece at the end of the early period. By this time, Akhenaton had repudiated almost all of the traditional gods of the Egyptian pantheon in favor of the Aton. While somewhat monotheistic in its emphasis of one god, there were tendencies of archaism as well—an attempt to recreate the absolute powers held by the pharaohs of the Fourth and Fifth Dynasties. Now, only Akhenaton and his family could worship the Aton directly; the people had to worship their god through their king.

Unfinished Relief
of an Amarna Princess

THIS LIMESTONE RELIEF shows techniques of sculpting used by the ancient Egyptian artists. After the scene was sketched and corrected, it was then carved. The princess depicted here sitting on a cushion has already been sculpted in a preliminary fashion. The outlines are still to be smoothed, and the area of the abdomen is the only part of the inner surface of the figure which has received its contours and details. The table, piled high with fruits, vegetables, and cakes, is shown only in outline drawing.

The realistic manner of execution and the limitation of exaggerated details would suggest a date late in Akhenaton's reign. Such a suggestion is supported by the provenience, since this trial piece was found in the North Palace at the site of Akhetaton.

The scene is reminiscent of part of a painted decoration on a wall of the king's house at Amarna which depicts two princesses seated similarly on a cushion. They are shown nude, however, while the figure illustrated here, owing to the indications on the neck and arms, appears to wear a diaphanous gown. She is eating a small duck, while reaching for a piece of fruit. A jug of wine rests beneath the table. It is possible that the relief was meant by the artist merely as a sketch, but it also may have been intended as a model or trial piece for decoration on a wall.

Relief from the Tomb of Aye

THIS CARVED LIMESTONE RELIEF comes from the Amarna tomb of the high official Aye. Aye stands before his wife Tiye, and they are below the window where royal appearances were made (not visible here) to receive gifts from the king. The necklace that is being offered is similar to the gold of favor which he already wears. Such an honor was bestowed by the king on important officials who had performed their duties particularly well. The conical objects on the heads of the two figures are perfume cones which were worn on a variety of occasions and would ensure the individual of always having a pleasant fragrance.

Since Aye had the title "God's Father," a designation often held by the father-in-law of the king, it has been suggested that he was the father of Nefertiti. A connection to the royal family has also been proposed since Aye's name is similar in spelling to that of Yuya who was also a "God's Father." He was the father of Amenhotep III's wife, Queen Tiye, and may also have been Aye's father.

Aye prepared his tomb at Akhetaton, but he outlived the religious revolution, figured prominently in the return to Thebes, and eventually, no doubt at an advanced age, succeeded Tutankhamun to the throne of Egypt. As most of his predecessors of the Eighteenth Dynasty, from Thutmosis I on, he made his final resting place in the Valley of the Kings.

Aye Before the Mummiform Figure of Tutankhamun

THE SCENE, SHOWING THE RECENTLY DECEASED FIGURE of Tutankhamun on the left being ministered to by the succeeding king, Aye, on the right, was painted on the eastern portion of the northern wall of the Burial Chamber in the tomb of Tutankhamun. The walls of this room were the only ones of the small tomb that were decorated.

Here, Aye, wearing the priestly leopard robe, performs the ceremony of "Opening the Mouth" before the mummy of the deceased Tutankhamun. With this ritual, which was to be repeated daily on the statues of the king, the mummy could regain faculties he had in life: speaking, eating, walking, etc. The tool in Aye's hand is an adze, usually used by sculptors and carpenters in the carving of wood, and is to be placed at the mouth of Tutankhamun. The king's costume and headdress are those of a god of the underworld, Osiris, with whom he is now identified. The inscriptions before the figures record the throne name, personal name, and epithets of both kings.

It is possible that this small tomb may have been intended originally for Aye, who was apparently one of the young king's advisors. He, like the nonroyal parents of Queen Tiye, Yuya and Thuya, would have been granted special permission to have a tomb in the Valley of the Kings because of a close connection with the royal family. When Tutankhamun died, his own tomb may not have been ready owing to his untimely death, and his successor, Aye, could provide him with his smaller but nearly complete tomb. Aye, then, who was buried in a tomb more typical of those of the other pharaohs of the Eighteenth Dynasty, may have completed and used the tomb originally begun for Tutankhamun.

Tutankhamun on a Lotus

LIKE MANY OF THE OBJECTS IN TUTANKHAMUN'S TOMB, this wooden life-size head covered with gesso (plaster) and then painted reflects elements of the orthodox religion reinstituted by the king. Here, however, the king is represented as a child, according to the small size of the head and the appearance of the features. All of the elements of the composition relate to a myth involving the young sun god.

Despite the fact that several theories existed simultaneously in ancient Egypt to describe the origin of the universe, it appears that all the concepts begin with primordial water. In one cosmological explanation, a lotus emerges on a mound in the water, and the infant sun god was born upon this flower. He then brings light to the land with his two eyes. This creation myth was accepted by some ancient theologians as the explication for the disappearance of the sun every evening and its reappearance the next morning. It was, in effect, reborn every day.

When the king died he often associated himself with particular gods, one of the most important of which was the sun god. In this sculpture, Tutankhamun is identified with the sun god, and, therefore, he too will be reborn every morning. Such compositions are not infrequent, and Ramesses II had himself depicted as the infant sun god on a pendant for a necklace.

The god Nefertem is often pictured with the lotus as well. Despite the fact that in one set of doctrines, he is the son of Ptah and Sekhmet, he is also regarded as the youthful sun god. In such as association, the sculpture may represent Tutankhamun as Nefertem, an embodiment of the newborn sun.

Carter unearthed this object from the rubble used to fill the Entrance Corridor; it was not in the tomb itself. It is likely, therefore, that the robbers discarded it in their hasty exit. The jewelry that probably once adorned the head was stolen in antiquity, but the remnants of an earring still remains intact in the left ear. Only the back button and post still exist; the other parts and the right earring were stolen or destroyed over three thousand years ago.

Child's Chair

BECAUSE OF ITS SMALL SCALE (less than thirty inches high), this wooden chair was considered by Carter to have been used by Tutankhamun as a child. The death of the king at so young an age might have been the impetus for the inclusion among his funerary equipment of a number of items that were used during his early childhood. That would also explain the placement of a bracelet encrusted with a large lapis lazuli scarab among the personal objects stored in a chest in the Treasury.

In form, the chair, which came from the Antechamber, is similar to contemporaneous examples (page 17). It is almost identical in size to a small chair of Sitamun, although the decoration on her chair is much more elaborate than on Tutankhamun's chair. The legs are feline in form, and the back is braced by three vertical supports. Most of the wood is ebony, but the slats of the seat appear to be made of rosewood, and this may be, therefore, one of the earliest extant examples of that wood. The back, like that of the inlaid chair (see page 61) has vertical panels of ivory. Two horizontal bands of stylized floral petals, also made of ivory, surmount the panels. Several rows of ivory and ebony inlays arranged in a geometric pattern border the entire back.

The arms have panels of carved and gilded gesso. Decorated with a recumbent oryx on each of the outer sides, the panels depict a floral motif within a border on the inner sides. Carved ivory terminals in the shape of lotuses serve as a crosspiece between the legs of the chair. In addition, vertical and diagonal pieces brace the legs. Unlike the inlaid chair (page 61), the golden throne (page 63), and the carved wooden chair (page 67), the child's chair has no inscription anywhere.

Ostrich Feather Fan

IN THE BURIAL CHAMBER Carter discovered this fan, one made of ebony, a longbow, and arrows. These objects were placed between the third and fourth (innermost) shrines that enclosed the sarcophagus, coffins, and mummy of the king. *In situ,* but now no longer extant, were the remains of thirty ostrich feathers, alternating white and brown. Made of wood and covered in sheet gold, the fan was about four feet in length without the feathers. The semicircular holder with the plumes intact would have looked similar to a palm leaf, but the handle terminates in a papyrus at the bottom and what appears to be a stylized papyrus (or perhaps a lotus) at the top. An inscription engraved on the handle includes, as well as epithets of the king, information that the king secured the plumes during a hunting trip in the desert, east of the city of Heliopolis.

The scene depicted on the front shows the king in his chariot hunting the ostrich from which the feathers would be obtained for the fan. The reverse side portrays the return from the fray, with two attendants in front of the royal chariot carrying the subdued ostriches. In the scene pictured here, we do not see the convention of portraying the bowstring behind (to the far side of) the face, as was the case on the golden shrine (page 55) and the elaborately decorated chest (page 73). The inscription before him states: "The good God, 'Ra is the Lord of Manifestations,' Given Life, like Ra forever, Lord of Power." Behind him is the wish that "All protection of/and life be behind him." At the far left, rather than a servant, an anthropomorphized *ankh* carries a fan similar to the one illustrated here, and it indicates, as do frequent representations of such fans in use, that they function mainly as sunshades.

Detail of Elaborately Decorated Chest

ALTHOUGH CHESTS WERE COMMONLY PLACED in tombs, judging from the physical evidence and the representations on the walls, no other example showed such skill and artistry in both construction and decoration. The Egyptians generally used chests for storage, and, although this piece was empty when Carter found it in the Annex, originally it probably contained clothing of the king. The architectonic design with cavetto cornice is similar to that of the more vertically oriented golden shrine (page 55). When placed atop the chest, the lid would have been secured in place by a cord around the knob pictured here and one on the lid itself.

Made of a red wood, almost every part of the outer surface is either inlaid, gilded, covered, or veneered. Ebony, ivory, faience, calcite, and gilt are the materials that richly decorate the surface and adhere to it by means of glue and, in a few cases, copper nails.

In the center, surrounded by borders of stained ivory, is a scene depicting the king and queen in the marshes. Tutankhamun sits on a cushion on a chair while shooting arrows into the thicket before him. Fish are depicted in the pool, while birds flutter around the vegetation. Ankhesanamun, seated on a cushion at his feet, holds his next arrow in her left hand, while an attendant in the lower right retrieves a speared fish and bird. A similar, but much less cluttered scene, is embossed on the left side of the golden shrine (page 55). The string of the bow in both cases passes, not in front of, but behind the face of the king, unlike the bowstring used by Tutankhamun in the ostrich hunt (page 33).

The royal couple, portrayed in the informal attitudes introduced during the Amarna period, is relaxing in a lush garden. The floral motif is continued in the other decorative panels, which depict a variety of animals in pursuit of their prey. The lid shows the queen offering flowers to the king, while below them attendants are plucking flowers.

Model Boomerang

CARTER FOUND MANY WEAPONS, such as bows, arrows, throw sticks, and boomerangs, in the Annex of the tomb. Along with these real instruments were models. This boomerang, found in a box with several wooden ones, is one such model. Carved of ivory and capped in gold, it would be too delicate for frequent use, and the flat terminal is atypical for a boomerang. The inscription refers to Tutankhamun as "the God, Lord of the Two Lands, 'Ra is the Lord of Manifestations,' Beloved of Ptah, Who is South of his Wall."

The boomerang was used in ancient Egypt in all periods primarily to hunt fowl in the marshes. Scenes of tomb owners, about to hurl the weapon, were part of the artists' repertoire as early as the Old Kingdom (2700-2150 B.C.). A depiction of the king hunting is on the left side of the golden shrine (page 55). There, Tutankhamun stands in a papyrus skiff in the marshes, the boomerang in his right hand and captured birds in his left. While this scene may reflect an activity which he hoped to include in his Afterlife, it is possible that the action of hunting the fowl may represent the king triumphing over the evil denizens of the marsh. The model boomerang then would have magical significance as a ritual weapon to aid Tutankhamun in overcoming the obstacles he would face in his voyage to the Afterlife.

Model Boat

Tutankhamun's tomb contained several different types of model boats, some of which were related to the funeral, some to the Afterlife, and some to mythical voyages. Fourteen of these craft were found in the Treasury, while still more were discovered in the Annex in a badly damaged state.

The model boat pictured here, found in the Treasury, is made of wood, part of which is covered with gesso (plaster) and then painted. The bow, stern, steering oars, and throne are gilded. The terminals of both the bow and the stern are carved in the shape of papyri. Close to the bow is a painted representation of the eye of Horus. The two oars attached to vertical posts with a cross piece are the steering mechanism. In the center is a gilded chair whose shape and decorative motifs—the feather pattern and the heraldic plants of Upper and Lower Egypt—indicate that it was a throne.

Unlike many of the other model boats in the tomb, there are no cabins or windscreens for the passenger. This craft was not part of the funerary cortege nor was it like one of the ships which the pharaoh used in life. One of four similar boats, all of which apparently related to the journey of the sun god, this craft was used to convey the king on his voyage with the sun god during the twelve hours of the night. Representations of similar vessels can be seen in vignettes of funerary papyri.

Model Boat with Rigging

UNLIKE THE MODEL BOAT (page 39) that the king was to use during his journey through the Afterlife, this ship was a model of a royal craft that was used during the king's lifetime. It has the original double mast, and when Carter recorded it in the Treasury the lowered square sail made of linen dyed red was still in place. The cabin in the center is painted in a checkerboard pattern, and there are stairs leading to the roof. Doors have been omitted, and the captured enemies usually represented on the sides of the stairway are barely visible. Geometric and floral motifs are painted on the front and back of the hull.

The two steering rudders are tied into place against two vertical supports braced by a crosspiece. Each of the rudders ends on top with a carved and gilded head complete with an elaborate crown and beard. The body of the ship is carved from a single log and comes to a point at the bow and a flattened" fishtail" at the stern. There are two gilded booths: one with an openwork sphinx carved on either side is at the front, while a bull adorns the shrine at the back. These elaborately carved open booths have a roof supported by four columns, and the royal insignia of the sphinx and bull are placed less than halfway up the sides.

The Nile was a highway for the ancient Egyptians, and boats such as these frequently sailed upstream. Since sails would be unnecessary for the trip downstream, the tomb of Tutankhamun was also provided with ships without rigging.

The King as Harpooner

CARVED IN WOOD, the figure was gessoed and gilded. The ends of the painted papyrus skiff were also gilded. The harpoon which the king holds in his right hand and the coiled rope in his left are made of bronze, like the slippers he wears, the uraeus (serpent) attached to his crown, and the inlaid eyebrows.

On the walls of many private tombs both before and during the New Kingdom, the owner is often shown on a small raft fowling or fishing in the marshes. While the action illustrated by this statue is similar, the king hunts neither fish nor fowl, but the hippopotamus, the animal sacred to the god Seth. Like many other objects in the tomb, it relates to the traditional religion restored by Tutankhamun. Since the king is the embodiment of the falcon god Horus, the figure is a three-dimensional representation of the conflict between Horus and Seth, a mythical confrontation between these two gods. This statue, found in the Treasury, was one of a pair, and both, covered with linen, were inside a darkly varnished chest. Neither one, however, contained the hippopotamus of Seth, the enemy of Horus's father, Osiris. The omission of the hippopotamus is not accidental; it was never meant to be part of the composition. Seth being understood as an evil deity, his presence, even as an animal, in the royal tomb would constitute a threat to the king; so his absence was deliberate.

The elegance of the carving and the grace of the figure is almost unparalleled in Egyptian art. Although more naturalistic than its predecessors, the art of the Amarna period tended often to the extremes. This piece illustrates the best characteristics of the Amarna period, balanced with the restraint characterized by Tutankhamun's reign. The uniqueness of the figure is not limited to the style, but extends also to the composition itself. Although similar representations can be found in two dimensions, three-dimensional representations of royal figures in such an active pose are extremely rare.

Painted Wooden Chest

ONE OF THE MOST INTRICATELY DECORATED OBJECTS in the tomb, this wooden chest, which was found in the Antechamber, illustrates the innovation of the frenzied battle. A fierce confrontation takes place on both sides of the box; pictured here is the king in his chariot fighting against the Asiatics. On the other side the king battles against the Nubians (page 47). Scenes such as these were the apparent influence for the artists who composed the military reliefs for the pharaohs of the Nineteenth Dynasty, where the enemy is also frequently depicted as a confused mass without the traditional registers. The absence of these groundlines make possible the chaotic disarray of the enemy. Chaos and disorder were anathema to the ancient Egyptian, since they represented the opposites of *maat*, the balance and harmony upon which the entire culture was based. These battle scenes, therefore, appear to have symbolic significance.

The curved lid is divided into two sections, each of which has a horizontal panel portraying the king pursuing wild animals. The smaller sides each have two representations of Tutankhamun as a sphinx treading upon his enemies.

On the long horizontal panel here, the king shoots his arrows into the fray. Behind him are three registers of subordinate personnel. The inscription before Tutankhamun refers to him as: "The good god, the Son of Amon, the Valiant one, without his equal, A Possessor of strength who tramples hundreds of thousands, who makes them into a pile of corpses." Both his throne name, Nebkheperura, and his personal name, Tutankhamun, appearing under the designation, the "good god, Son of Ra," are written in front of him.

Detail of the Painted Wooden Chest

THE SCENE DEPICTED HERE, like the rest of the decoration (see page 45), is painted on the smooth gesso covering the wood. The Nubians are scattering as the pharaoh charges into battle. The vivid portrayal is rendered in such detail that it is possible to see the trappings of the horses, the markings on the animals, the varied patterns of the Nubians' shields, and the pained expressions on the individuals being ravaged by the pharaoh's hounds. Below the horses, a decapitated enemy falls, and his head topples to the ground. Behind the king run a trio of fan bearers (page 33), while directly overhead is the disk of the sun with two cobras wearing *ankhs* protruding on either side. The protective vulture goddess, Nekhbet, hovers both before and behind the king, and the hieroglyphic sign for heaven *(pet)* extends across only the part of the scene depicting the chariot.

The inscription states: "The good god, Image of Ra, Who appears upon the foreign lands like the rising of Ra, He who destroys this vile land of Kush (Nubia), He who shoots his arrows against the enemies." While Tutankhamun was frequently portrayed as a warrior, it is not known for certain whether he actually took part in any battles. Despite the fact that the general Horemhab apparently controlled the military affairs for his king, Tutankhamun certainly would have been capable of engaging in military activity by his early teens. In addition, the family into which he was born boasted of great prowess in archery, and he certainly enjoyed spending his leisure time hunting with bow and arrow (page 35).

Red Gold Plaque
with Openwork Design

THIS SMALL TINTED GOLD PLAQUE, which may have functioned as a buckle, is less than four inches wide and three inches high. It has a reddish cast because it has been tinted with a microscopically thin layer of what may be an iron derivative. The background has been cut away, leaving a skillfully crafted openwork design. It depicts the king returning triumphantly from battle, his captured prisoners before him. The necks of the Nubian and the Asiatic are tied with a rope, one end of which ends with a lotus (symbolic of Upper Egypt) and the other with a papyrus (symbolic of Lower Egypt). Underneath the horses and chariot is the symbolic representation of the unification of Upper and Lower Egypt, as in the legs of the inlaid chair (page 61). Flanking the hieroglyph for unification, in the center, is a Syrian on the left and a Nubian on the right. Facing each prisoner is a heraldic plant, which unlike those binding the figures, does not correspond to the geographic location of the homeland of the captives; they may relate instead to the protective goddesses above.

Nekhbet, the vulture goddess of Upper Egypt, faces Tutankhamun and offers him the hieroglyph for "life," *ankh*. Behind the king is the serpent Wadjet of Lower Egypt who rests on a clump of papyrus. She holds a cartouche engraved with the throne name of the king, "Ra is the Lord of Manifestations," while under her wing is the wish that "All life of/and protection be behind him like Ra forever." Despite the fact that a ritual rather than an actual battle was represented on this plaque, the presence in the tomb of military equipment indicates at least some familiarity on the part of the king with objects of warfare. According to Carter, the piece was found in the Antechamber in a small chest which included also a priestly robe, a gilded leopard head, a large gold and lapis lazuli scarab, and a scepter.

Votive Shield

THIS SHIELD IS ONE OF EIGHT that Carter found in the Annex. Boomer-angs, throw-sticks, bows, and arrows were also among the military equipment stored in this room. Although this elaborately decorated object, like three similar shields, was never meant for use in life, four of the shields clearly were battle-worthy. Made of wood and covered in animal hide, they were slightly smaller in size than the ceremonial versions. The four larger shields were constructed similarly in that the background of each composition was cut away, leaving an openwork design (page 49). Each was made of wood that was smoothed with gesso and then gilded.

On the front of the shield Tutankhamun triumphantly brandishes a scimitar in his right hand and holds the tails of his foes, two lions, in his left. Representations of the king smiting enemies had already become a standard theme in Egyptian art, and the artist here is recreating a traditional motif, albeit with some modifications, that had already been in existence for more than fifteen hundred years. Behind him, the Upper Egyptian vulture goddess, Nekhbet, spreads her protective wings about him. The basket upon which she perches rests on the plant symbolic of Lower Egypt, the papyrus. The winged sun disk hovers over the whole scene, while the king is about to slay the lions, which considering the context should be understood as symbolic representations of his traditional enemies. Aside from the usual epithets, the hieroglyphic inscription likens the king to the warlike god of Thebes, Montu.

Two Daggers and Sheaths of the King

WHEN THE BURIAL CHAMBER HAD BEEN EMPTIED to the point that the excavators could open the innermost coffin, they found the intact mummy of the king. In the process of unwrapping it and examining the body, they discovered two daggers on his person. On the right side of the abdomen beneath a golden waistband was the golden dagger (upper part of the plate), and wrapped to the right thigh of Tutankhamun was the second dagger (lower part of the plate). Both daggers and sheaths are similar in design, and the handles of both are decorated mainly with bands of geometric patterns in granulated gold alternating with rows mainly of floral designs inlaid with colored glass and semiprecious stones. Two falcons are inlaid on the uppermost band of the hilt of the golden dagger, while the knob of the other dagger is made of rock crystal. The sheath of the golden dagger has an elaborately inlaid featherlike pattern on one side and an intricately embossed surface depicting lions, dogs, and a leopard attacking their prey on the other. The sheath of the other dagger is much simpler in design with a detailed floral pattern engraved in rather low relief on one side, and a simple feathered design on the other.

The blades of the two daggers are quite distinct. That of the golden dagger is simple in its design, but that of the other knife has no discernible decoration. Its distinction is that it is made of nonmeteoric iron which, until this time, was unknown in Egypt. Apparently a Hittite import into Egypt, it is among only a few other objects of the same material which were also near the mummy of Tutankhamun. Both the iron blade and the decorative motifs, such as the rows of animals and the spiral patterns on the sheath of the golden dagger, are not native to Egypt. Such factors may indicate foreign production of these daggers. It is more likely, however, that they were made in Egypt and that the foreign elements can be attributed either to the hand of a foreign craftsman in Egypt or to the cosmopolitan repertoire of an Egyptian artisan.

Golden Shrine

THIS WOODEN SHRINE, covered in sheet gold, rests on a sledge covered in silver. Found in the Antechamber of the tomb of Tutankhamun, it originally contained a statuette, judging from the presence of an empty pedestal carved with two footprints. Made of a precious metal, the figure, most likely that of the king, was probably stolen in one of the two attempts to rob the tomb in antiquity. The shape of the shrine is one which can be traced back to the earliest period of Egyptian history.

The lid is decorated with elements of the traditional religion that Tutankhamun restored: the vulture goddess, Nekhbet, a winged disk of Horus, and a winged uraeus. It rests upon the cavetto cornice of the shrine. All around the surface, in low, raised relief are scenes depicting mainly the intimacy between the king and his wife Ankhesenamun. There are portrayals of the king at leisure, hunting, fowling, and being anointed, and the queen always accompanies him. There are, however, a few portrayals that refer to the coronation of the king, such as the presentation of the necklace by the queen, visible on the upper left portion of the right side. It is noteworthy that although the king is shown wearing a variety of crowns and headdresses, he wears neither the white crown of Upper Egypt nor the double crown. Such an omission is interesting considering the frequent representation of the protective goddess of Upper Egypt, Nekhbet, such as fourteen depictions of her on the roof. Moreover, the shape of the shrine is similar to that of the ancient pavilion of Nekhbet. Names and designations of the king and queen are inscribed on the borders.

Detail from the Golden Shrine

THE GOLD OVERLAY ON WHICH THE SCENES ARE EMBOSSED rests on a layer of linen and gesso that has the same carved design. It was apparently applied in a semiliquid state to the back of the gold and allowed to harden. The entire compound was then applied to the wooden surface of the shrine with another layer of linen, to help prevent damage to the exposed surface of the design.

In this panel, the king sits on a cushion on a folding stool similar to a model of such a seat found in the tomb (page 59) except that the legs here are in the form of feline paws. In his left hand he holds two flowers; he pours liquid from a vessel in his right hand for his wife who cups her right hand to receive it. She sits on a cushion at his feet, which are raised up on a footstool. The informality of the scene is another innovation of the Amarna period that persists into the reign of Tutankhamun.

Ankhesenamun wears an elaborate crown (page 65), and the inscription above her refers to her as "The Great King's wife, Lord of the two lands, Ankhesenamun. May she live forever." In front of the king's head is his throne name, while his personal name is behind. He wears the blue crown, the so-called war crown, from which flutter two streamers. The inscription on the far right, which is part of the text bordering all the scenes, states: "Nebkheperura, Son of Ra, His beloved, Lord of appearances, Tutankhamun." The Amon names of both the king and queen have been altered from their earlier Aton names.

Model of a Folding Stool

THIS STOOL FROM THE ANTECHAMBER reflects the close ties that Egypt had with Nubia during the reign of Tutankhamun, since a similar stool is depicted on the wall of the tomb of one of Tutankhamun's officials, Huy. He led an expedition to Nubia and brought back the chair represented on his wall as tribute for his king. By imitating such a chair in ebony, ivory, and gold, materials which all came from Nubia, the implicit connection with Nubia was made. It is even possible that Tutankhamun wished to have a representative of Nubian tribute that would magically always be present in his Afterlife.

Although this example is fixed in its position, it is a model of the type of portable stool that could be used in a variety of environments (page 57). The legs, ending in the heads of fowl, are similar to those on the inlaid chair (page 61) and the stained ivory headrest (page 95), and the crosspieces are held in the mouths of the birds. The seat itself is fashioned of ebony, and it has inlays of ivory. Every attempt was made to copy the original model, and the golden-tipped tail of the imitation skin, attached to a midline fashioned of a red wood, dangles toward the ground. Gold tips are on the ends of the crosspieces and cover the middle part of the legs.

The four corners of the seat are damaged, and it has been suggested that originally there were golden claws there that were pulled from the stool by the robbers. The probable presence of claws has led to the suggestion that the skin being imitated is that of a leopard rather than a cow. The reverse coloration is due to the difficulty of using ivory over a large area. Such an explanation, however, does not account for the gold still remaining on the legs and the strange shape of the tail.

Inlaid Chair

FOUND IN THE ANNEX AMIDST A GROUP of domestic furniture, this elaborately inlaid wooden chair was considered by Carter to have been most likely a "chair of state" or an "ecclesiastical throne." In form, the chair is a composite, uniting the curved seats of ordinary stools, the legs of folding stools, and the back, with its three vertical supports, of chairs commonly found in the New Kingdom and before. The crossed legs ending in the heads of fowl are parallel to the legs of an imitation folding stool found in the Antechamber. The borders of the seat, made of ebony, inlaid with ivory, imitate the hide of an animal, while the seat itself is composed of inlays of stained ivory arranged in panels imitating insets of a variety of skins. The underside of the seat is covered in real leather. The floral motif between the legs, damaged in one of the ancient intrusions into the tomb, is a frequently used heraldic element in chairs and stools.

The rectangular panels of the seat reflect the architectonic design on the back of the chair. Inlaid with ivory and ebony, they contain hieroglyphic inscriptions with designations of the king. The decoration on the upper portion and the borders includes sheet gold and inlays of colored glass, faience, and semiprecious stones. The chair itself, a hybrid of designs, contains references to the traditional religion of ancient Egypt: the goddess Nekhbet and the sacred eye of Horus are represented in gold on the reverse side of the back. Nekhbet can be seen also on the upper part of the seat, and above her is a frieze of serpents with the solar disk upon their heads. The majority of the inscriptions (all of the vertical ones) have the early name of the king, Tutankhaton; his later name, Tutankhamun, occurs as well (in the horizontal inscriptions). It appears that the chair must have been produced at the time when the traditional religion and that of the Aton coexisted. There are references to several gods of the Egyptian pantheon as well as to the Aton; the word "gods," which had been eliminated in strict Atonist religion, appears once again.

The Golden Throne

THE GOLDEN THRONE THAT HOWARD CARTER DISCOVERED in the Antechamber beneath the hippopotamus couch is similar to the chair belonging to Sitamun (page 17). The style was popular for royal chairs of the Eighteenth Dynasty. Instead of female torsos protruding from the seat, however, the more traditional lions are in their place. Carved of wood, the armchair is covered in gold, and there is some silver overlay as well. Colored glass, faience, calcite, and semiprecious stones are used for the inlays.

The carved plant motif between the feline-form legs has been removed by the robbers, but the delicate openwork design of the arms remains intact. On either side, a winged cobra wears the double crown and rests on a basket. Her outstretched wings enclose the hieroglyphs for the "King of Upper and Lower Egypt" followed by the sign for infinity (shen). A cartouche of the king is at the end of her wings on either side of the chair.

The back of the chair is supported by three vertical struts (pages 17 and 31); the outer two are carved with the king's Aton name, the middle one with that of the queen. Four hooded cobras with solar disks rise up in pairs between each of the supports. A carved and gilded scene with birds in a thicket appears on the outer surface of the back of the seat. In the triangular opening formed between the diagonal of the back and the vertical supports on each side is a hooded cobra. The one on the left wears the red crown of Lower Egypt, while the one on the right has the white crown of Upper Egypt.

The iconography relates to Atonist doctrines (page 65), but the names of the king and queen appearing on the chair use both the earlier (Aton) and later (Amon) forms. Such a combination indicates that the chair was probably produced rather early in Tutankhamun's reign, during the period of transition to the orthodox religion.

Detail from the Throne

THE SCENE SHOWN HERE is from the back of the throne (page 63). It depicts the young king seated at left, his feet upon an ottoman. Before him is his wife Ankhesenamun, who leans forward and touches his shoulder. The informality of the portrayal is typical of the Amarna period, and a similar scene can be found on the back of the golden shrine (page 57). The base of an unguent vessel, visible below the left hand of Ankhesenamun, is still intact, and it indicates that the young queen was anointing her husband. Between the two figures are the rays of the Aton which end in hands. The rays nearest to the noses of the royal pair extend *ankhs*. Such a scene, frequently represented during the Amarna period, is similar to that depicted in the painted stela (page 21). Despite such a clear reference to the religion of the Amarna period, the cartouche near his elaborate crown encircles his later name, Tutankhamun. His earlier name, Tutankhaton, however, occurs elsewhere on the chair.

Below the royal couple is an elaborate architectural motif, called a dado. Above the scene, at the top of the back of the chair, is a frieze of serpents each of which has a solar disk on its head. Clearly visible on the representation of the chair upon which Tutankhamun sits is the fretwork composed of the plants symbolic of Upper and Lower Egypt. This delicate decoration between the legs of the chair is similar to the partially destroyed fretwork on the inlaid chair (page 63). The vertical supports for the back of the chair can be seen clearly in this representation (compare the chair of Sitamun, page 17). Behind the queen are floral garlands.

Wooden Chair

SOMETIMES REFERRED TO AS THE "CEREMONIAL CHAIR" because of its decoration, this chair has the basic style of armless chairs of the New Kingdom. Like the golden throne (pages 63 and 65), it too comes from the Antechamber. The wood, however, is reddish, resembling a coniferous type native to Lebanon. Sheet gold embossed with a spiral design covers the curved braces between the seat and back; the same material is used for the winged sun disk. Round gold caps, arranged symmetrically, cover several dowels.

The carved openwork design of the back is of the highest artistic quality found in ancient Egypt. In the central portion, the god Heh kneels upon a hieroglyph for "gold" *(nebu)*. In each hand he grasps the hieroglyph for "year" *(renpet)* which rests on a tadpole, meaning "a hundred thousand" *(hefen)*, and the sign for "infinity" *(shen)*. Around his left arm dangles the hieroglyph for the word "life," *ankh* (page 91). The composition symbolizes the hope that the king will reign for eternity.

The two horizontal panels directly in front of and behind Heh, flanking the solar disk, contain a reference to the king and his cartouche. The larger panels surmounted by the falcon with a double crown and cobras have the Horus name of the king, one of the several designations that he possessed (page 129), and on the bottom is the traditional *serekh*, the two-dimensional rendering of the palace facade. The bands of inscription bordering the back give several epithets of the king as well as references to him in relation to the traditional gods. On the other side of the back, there are epithets on the borders and in the three vertical supports. The openwork design is repeated here as well, but the inscriptions on the four vertical panels, which in the front are carved in raised relief, are here rendered in sunk relief.

The Crook of the King

MOST OF THE OTHER OBJECTS IN THE TOMB that reflected the activities of the king (pages 33 and 67) were readily visible to Carter. The crook, however, lay hidden in a chest in the Antechamber along with several other objects, such as the red gold plaque with openwork design (page 49). It was not until he emptied the chest in the laboratory that he realized the value of its contents. Included also were gold rings (page 115), collars, necklaces, a golden scarab, a priestly robe, and a gilded wooden head of a leopard traditionally worn with the robe.

The crook has a core of bronze over which are alternating bands of blue glass and gold. Each of the two caps has the king's throne name, Nebkheperura, written on it. Traditionally, the crook was held in one hand (usually the left) of the ruling king, while the flail was grasped in the other (page 89), although the two could also be held in one hand. These symbols of kingship were also held by the god Osiris in his role as ruler of the Underworld (page 27), and when the king was identified with him, he carried them as well (page 45).

The crook itself, when written as a hieroglyph, means "ruler" (*heka*), and this usage probably derives from the fact that it was held by the king. Although the crook was not found with its companion, the flail, two pairs of flails and crooks were found in the Treasury. One of the flails, inscribed with the early name of the king, Tutankhaton, is similar in size to the crook illustrated here.

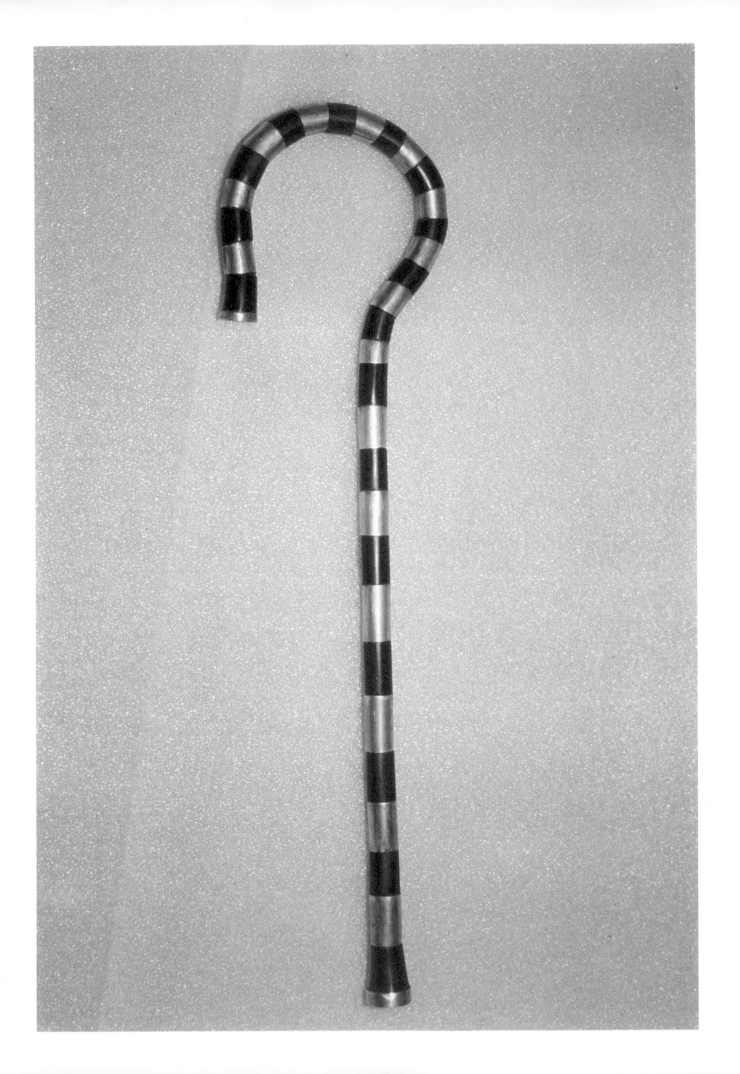

Two Game Boards

ASIDE FROM CONTAINING MILITARY EQUIPMENT, the Annex held, among all the funerary equipment strewn about in great disarray, several objects that appeared to be there for the young king's amusement. There were implements for hunting and archery, and there were mechanical toys and games. Illustrated here are two of the four gaming boards that were found in the tomb. Although their presence indicates Tutankhamun's predilection for the game while still alive, it also implies their use in the Afterlife. Several representations on the walls of New Kingdom tombs show the game being played, and the seventeenth chapter of the Book of the Dead (a collection of funerary spells used by the deceased from the time of the New Kingdom on to insure their entry into the Afterlife) states that the game of Senet ("Passing") would be played by the deceased upon going forth into the next world. All four gaming boards found in the tomb were capable of actual use, and those which are illustrated in the foreground are the two largest.

The smaller of these is covered with stained ivory. The sides have a floral pattern similar to that on the elaborately decorated chest (pages 73 and 35), and there are two drawers for storage of the gaming pieces. There are thirty squares on the board; another board is on the reverse side with fewer squares.

The larger board is much more formal in appearance. The table on which it rests is supported by animal-shaped legs like those of some chairs (page 17). It is placed upon a sledge. It had only one drawer whose length would allow it to be used for storage. Most of the gaming pieces for this board were missing, and Carter assumed that they were probably made of a precious metal and were stolen in antiquity. The stand and sledge are ebony and the board is veneered with the same wood; the boards are inlaid with ivory. The reverse side has only twenty squares, and the game Tjau ("Thieves") was played on it. Titles and epithets of the king are inscribed in a band around the box and the drawer.

Elaborately Decorated Chest

THIS ELABORATE CHEST, a detail of which has already been illustrated (page 35), was found by Carter in the Annex. The chest had already been ransacked when the officials of the necropolis restored order to the tomb. Since neither wardrobes nor closets were in use in Egypt until much later, boxes like these, varying in size and design, often served the same purpose. The detailed treatment of the outer surface of this piece suggests that it contained garments for ceremonial occasions.

The long horizontal decorative panel is bordered by alternately colored red and blue inlays, between which are plaques with vertical inlays of ivory and ebony. Both this and a similar band on the ledge of the chest may be an imitation of colorful reed matting. Below this is a border in a checkerboard pattern under which is another band, this time in a pattern of stylized petals made of white ivory. Surrounding the scene in the center, and extending outward at the top, are two white ivory inlays, between which is one band of ebony. The central panel, divided into five parts, portrays several bovines, some in flight and others recumbent, and a lion pursuing an ibex. Details of landscape surround the creatures whose style is similar to that on the sheath of the golden dagger (page 53).

Bordering the scene on three sides are several separate floral groupings similar to the decoration in ivory veneer on the sides of the smaller of the two game boards (page 71).

Chest with Applied Gilded Decoration

SEVERAL BOXES WERE PLACED NEXT TO EACH OTHER on the north side of the Treasury. One of the most elaborately decorated of these is illustrated here. The basic wood structure was, according to Carter, cedar. The ivory knobs were stained red. Horizontal and vertical bands of ivory were applied to all four sides and the lid, and a hieroglyphic inscription giving the formal names of the king, which he received at his coronation, were incised and then filled in with black pigment. The queen's name is also recorded on the bands.

The spacing of the ivory bands leaves open several horizontal panels on each of the sides and the lid. In these spaces is an openwork design in carved and gilded wood. Applied to the wood, these golden hieroglyphs, *ankh, was,* and *neb,* mean "all life and dominion" (page 111). In the six panels on the roof, the hieroglyphs are arranged in trios, an *ankh* flanked by a *was* sign, and underneath is a *neb* basket. The hieroglyphs on the sides, however, are not as symmetrically arranged. Each of the four legs is capped in silver. The interior of the box has sixteen small compartments, and each division was edged in ivory.

Because of the small size of the inner partitions, Carter surmised that the original contents were gold or silver cosmetic jars. All had been stolen in antiquity, and the necropolis officials, who restored order to the tomb, utilized the chest for objects of lesser value, such as a basket and some scribal equipment.

Cabinet with Hieroglyphic Fretwork

THE ORIGINAL CONTENTS, which Carter thought might have been fine linen, were stolen in antiquity, but the necropolis officials who replaced the piece in the Annex stored four headrests in it. Unlike most of the other cabinets in Tutankhamun's tomb, whose lids are fixed in place by means of a tongue and groove construction, the lid of this piece can be opened and closed by the bronze hinges attached to the back of the chest. As was the case with the others, a cord would be wrapped around the gilded wooden knobs, and a seal would be impressed in wet clay.

The style is typical of Egyptian furniture, and it can be traced back over one thousand years. The legs supporting Tutankhamun's cabinet are longer and thinner than most examples of the same design and account for its elegant appearance. Composed of ebony, they extend upward and form the framework for the chest; the panels on the sides and the lid are of a reddish-brown wood that may be cedar. A hieroglyphic inscription, incised and filled with a yellow pigment, covers most of the ebony bands, but it does not extend to the legs. The phrases and epithets refer to the king and his relationship to the traditional pantheon; the Aton, however, is also mentioned.

The openwork design of the fretwork takes the form of a hieroglyphic inscription; *ankh* and *was* are the vertical signs, and *neb* is the horizontal sign—the *ankh* is ebony, and the others are gilded wood. "All life and dominion" is the phrase that is repeated around the chest, and it is the same that occurs on the chest with applied gilded decoration. Hieroglyphs were often used as a decorative motif on both furniture and jewelry, but they also served the purpose of communicating a message.

Unguent Vase with Plants
in Openwork Design

SEVERAL ELABORATELY CARVED VASES such as this were found in the Antechamber, but still others were discovered in the Annex. It was Carter's suggestion that the Annex may have been the original provenience for most of them, but that several were moved in the thieves' attempts to steal their contents.

This highly decorative piece was made from two blocks of calcite. The base depicts an anthropomorphized *ankh* on either side of the jar stand; it grasps the hieroglyph, *was* ("dominion"), in each hand. The vase itself is part of an overall design signifying the "unification of Upper and Lower Egypt," taking the place of the hieroglyph *sema* ("Unification"). Compare the motif on the fretwork of the inlaid chair (page 61). The plants, symbolic of Upper (lotus) and Lower (papyrus) Egypt, are on the left and right, respectively. They are tied about the neck of the vase. Completing the outer edge of the openwork handle is the notched palm branch signifying the Egyptian word for 'year,' *renpet.* Below each is the hieroglyphic sign for infinity surmounted by the Egyptian designation for one hundred thousand, the tadpole. The motif, therefore, represents "uncountable years." The king's cartouches written below the epithets, "Son of Ra, the Lord of the Two Lands," are placed within a rectangular outline, below which extends a carved band of stylized vegetation. A garland is at the base of the neck, while the head of the goddess Hathor (with the ears of a cow) is carved just below the rim of the vessel. Not visible here are two breasts in raised relief under the garland.

While it is clear that the artist wished to create a balanced composition, one side is not a mirror image of the other. Different plants are used on each side. In addition, the papyrus blossom (right) turning in toward the neck is attached to it, while the lotus blossom (left) remains free from the neck. It is highly unlikely that this inconsistency was an error, considering the high level of artistic competency exhibited in the design and execution of the vase.

Unguent Jar in the Form
of a Standing Lion

FOUND IN THE ANNEX, this jar was one of the more than fifty vessels in the tomb. Made of calcite like the others, it is distinguished by its form which has the shape of a lion; its head and body, which were hollowed out, held the unguent. The crown functioned either as a stopper or projecting neck and mouth for the jar. Unlike the many other containers in the tomb, this one still retained its contents, despite the fact that the crown had been detached in antiquity. The pedestal on which it stands is similar in design to contemporaneous jar stands and stools, and the bands of incised decoration are reminiscent of the borders of checkerboard pattern and stylized flower petals on the elaborately decorated chest (page 73).

The support for his left paw takes the shape of the Egyptian hieroglyph *sa* ("protection"), and this fact reinforces the identification of the lion with the god Bes (see the representation of him on the arm of the chair of Sitamun, (page 17). His claws, apparently inlaid in ivory or gold, are no longer intact; the dew claw, a vestigial part of the paw, which is also indicated on the two front animal-form legs of chairs, is shown in raised relief on his right paw. His eyes are gilded, and his teeth and tongue are of ivory. A hole was carved in each ear for earrings, but neither one has survived.

The inscription carved on his chest was filled in with colored pigment as was the case with the decoration on the crown and the base. It reads, "The Good God, the Lord of the Two Lands, 'Ra is the Lord of Manifestations,' 'Tutankhamun'; the Wife of the King, 'Ankhesenamun.'"

Unguent Container
with Crouching Lion on the Lid

CARVED OF TRANSLUCENT CALCITE, this vessel lay before the sealed doors of the second shrine in the Burial Chamber. Its contents, almost a pound of which survived, were chemically analyzed and found to consist of ninety percent animal fat with the remainder being either balsam or resin.

Cylindrical in shape, the jar has a lid that is supported on two sides by miniature columns with lotiform capitals surmounted by heads of Bes (pages 17 and 81). The tongue, made of stained ivory, is parallel to that of the crouching lion on the lid. The lion, bearing the cartouche of the king, is a symbol for him. His ears, like those of other animals in the tomb, are pierced (pages 81 and 85), but the earrings no longer remain. The recumbent figure majestically poses over the traditional enemies of Egypt, Asiatics and Nubians. Carved of red and black stones respectively, the heads of the figures are attached to the crosspieces under the container as a symbol of pharaoh's perpetual domination.

The container has two borders; the dominant theme of the upper one is a stylized floral border, and the lower one takes the form of a dado, an architectural motif. Between them are incised scenes of animals attacking their prey (pages 53 and 73). The background is tinted a dark hue so that the plants and animals stand out. A lion attacking a bull predominates on both sides, and hounds attack an ibex in a subsidiary scene. The swirl pattern on the shoulder of the attacking lion represents the tuft of hair on the animal's shoulder. The same feature appears on the recumbent lion on the lid as well as on the unguent jar in the form of a lion (page 81).

Detail of a Vessel
in the Form of an Ibex

THE TOMB OF TUTANKHAMUN contained a few containers in the shape of animals (page 81), and this one, like the one in the shape of a lion, came from the Annex. While animal-form jars were produced in the early periods of Egyptian history, they do not regain their popularity until the latter part of the Eighteenth Dynasty.

Carved of a single piece of calcite, this vase takes the form of an ibex, whose body has been hollowed out to receive its contents. It rests on a low slab of calcite. The opening or mouth of the vessel is on the back of the creature. The oils that it contained were stolen in one of the robberies of the tomb, shortly after the tomb had been sealed.

To heighten the realism of the composition, actual ibex horns were attached to the head, but only one survives. It may have secondary carving to add to its effect. The eyes, inlaid into metal sockets, were formed of glass or crystal, and the details were painted on the underside. The protruding tongue is made of ivory, stained red (pages 81 and 83). The animal's markings and other features such as the hooves were painted on the surface, and a cartouche with the king's throne name appears on the left shoulder. The ears of the animal were pierced, but the earrings have not survived.

Front of a Carved Calcite Boat

THE MOST INTRICATELY CARVED of the calcite objects found in the Annex is this elaborate composition consisting of a base in the form of a chest, upon which are incised bands of floral and geometric patterns. The chest itself stands on four legs and has been partially hollowed out. From its center rises a trapezoidal support decorated with stalks of papyrus plants, and the boat rests upon it.

Here we see the bow of the boat, which takes the form of the head and neck of an ibex, and another ibex, facing the same way, forms the stern. While the ears of both animals were pierced, the left ear of the rear figure retained its earring. An incised and painted pattern on the hull of the boat parallels the pattern on the base. Around the necks of both animals is a collar consisting of inlays of gold and colored glass.

A figure of a seated female is carved at the front of the boat. Here, golden earrings, an armlet, and a bead bracelet are still intact, and her wig is carved from gray stone. She holds a stained ivory lotus in her left hand. Behind her is a canopy supported by four ornate columns each of which has four screen walls, which may represent as well a sarcophagus or a cabin. In shape, it is similar to the base of the composition, and it is decorated with floral as well as geometric patterns. It may have served as a container for oil or an unguent, but Carter did not record finding any substance remaining. He considered the piece an ornament or a centerpiece.

Not visible here is the rear of the object, where another figure stands at the stern and holds a sounding pole in both hands. This one is a female dwarf, and she too wears a wig carved of gray stone.

Like the horns of the vessel in the form of an ibex (page 89), those of both animals here are real ibex horns. The ibex on the prow still has its characteristic beard intact. The markings are painted, and the details of the eyes are painted on the underside of glass or crystal pieces. The throne name of the king and the personal names of both he and his wife are written on the front of the support.

Small Container in the Shape
of a Double Cartouche

ONCE THE EXCAVATORS had cleared the stone sarcophagus of the three coffins, nested one within the other, and the bier that supported them, they found some chips of wood, a wooden lever, and the container illustrated here. Like many of the calcite vessels in the tomb (pages 79 and 81), it originally held some type of unguent, judging from the residue that still remained inside.

The double golden containers rest on a silver platform around the border on which the hieroglyphs for "life" *(ankh)* and "dominion" *(was)* are incised. The embossing on the sides of the boxes each depict the god Heh, kneeling on a basket and grasping the notched palm branch. (Compare the handles on the chalice, page 91.) Both in front of and behind his head are cartouches of the king, while directly overhead his throne name, Nebkheperura ("Ra is the Lord of Manifestations"), is written without a cartouche, and the traditional beetle, meaning "manifestations" (or "images") is replaced by a winged beetle.

The larger inlays consist of colored glass, while the smaller ones are stone. Within the cartouches on each side is an image of the king seated on a basket *(heb)*. Above is a solar disk from which project hooded cobras wearing *ankhs* around their necks. On the side illustrated here the king wears the side lock of youth, which may be an indication of his age or his status. On the other side, he wears the khepresh crown (page 27) commonly worn by kings of the Eighteenth Dynasty. The face of one of these images is blackened and, if intentional, may be an attempt to indicate Tutankhamun's association with the god of the Underworld, Osiris, whose skin can be green, symbolizing perennial vegetation, or black, representing the fertile soil.

The hieroglyphs written in a cartouche should spell the name of a king. Here, however, they are written indirectly, in a cryptogram. Each element has been disguised or written in an alternate form. Instead of the simple disk of the sun meaning the god Ra, there is an elaborate solar emblem with serpents. In place of the *neb* basket meaning "Lord," there is a *heb* basket. Compare the same substitution (page 111). Rather than write the traditional beetle (note the substitution of the winged beetle mentioned above), which means "manifestations" or "images," the artist depicted several images of the king. In actuality, the double cartouches each have the throne name of the king, "Ra is the Lord of Manifestations."

Chalice in the Form
of a Lotus

CARTER REPORTED that he had to step over this cup, which lay in the doorway, in order to get into the Antechamber. The cup itself, in the form of a white lotus, has petals carved in delicate low relief around its surface. An inscription carved within a rectangular outline gives the throne and personal names of the king and also refers to him as: "Beloved of Amon, Lord of the Thrones of the Two Lands, and Lord of Heaven." The hieroglyphs along the rim are divided into two parts: one, giving the titulary of the king, begins with the falcon and reads left to right. The other inscription records an eloquent wish for long life: "May your *ka* (essential nature of an individual) live; May you spend millions of years, Oh, you who love Thebes, sitting with your face toward the north wind and your eyes beholding happiness."

This request led Carter to designate the piece as the "Wishing Cup." The message is carried further, however, extending even to the decoration of the handles. On either side an open flower is flanked by two buds. Atop the central element of each is the god of eternity, Heh, who also signified the number "one million." In each hand, he grasps the notched palm branch, the hieroglyph for "year" that rests on the tadpole ("one hundred thousand") and the sign for "infinity." (See also the unguent vase, page 79.) Carved and filled with pigment, the hieroglyph *ankh* ("life"), is held in the god's hands, and the composition symbolizes life eternal.

Headrest

CARTER FOUND FOUR HEADRESTS made of different materials in a chest in the Annex. From the inscription in hieratic (script writing) on a similar box, he suggested that both chests originally contained linen and that the headrests were put in when the officials of the necropolis discovered the robbery and restored order in the tomb.

This headrest is made of a turquoise glass, while the others were composed of plain ivory, stained ivory (page 95), and faience. It is constructed of two separate pieces that were joined by means of a wooden dowel. A sheet of gold embossed with a pattern of repeating hieroglyphs, *ankh* ("life") and *was* ("dominion"), conceals the joint.

The faience example found along with it is similar in design. The making of faience, which includes ground quartz in its composition, represents a much older technique, predating glassmaking by more than two thousand years. Glassmaking was not perfected until comparatively late in Egyptian history—around the beginning of the Eighteenth Dynasty. Smoother in its surface than faience, it could be opaque like the example of translucent blue glass (page 99).

Because of the delicate nature of the material it is unlikely that the headrest was made for actual use; it was probably put in the tomb for ritual purposes. The vertical inscription incised in the central support identifies Tutankhamun by his throne name: "The Good God, Lord of the Two Lands, 'Ra is the Lord of Manifestations,' given life like Ra."

Stained Ivory Headrest

EACH OF THE HEADRESTS THAT CARTER FOUND in the Annex is fairly distinctive in style and composition. One of them, however, is completely different from the others. Whereas the other three are characterized by a solid central support (page 93), the example illustrated here resembles a piece of furniture used for sitting rather than an object used to prop up the head. In fact, with its two pairs of crossed supports, it is very similar to contemporaneous folding stools. As is the case with the inlaid chair (page 61), which imitates the style of folding stools, the heads of fowl form the bottom part of each of the supports. The horizontal stabilizers are attached to the open beaks of the birds. Unlike the inlaid chair, however, there is no inlay or gilding on the legs.

The entire object is constructed of ivory, much of which is carved and stained. The area where the head was to rest is constructed of three horizontal pieces that are alternately colored black and white. Attached to these, and curving upward on each side is a carved representation of the god Bes. Frequently represented on furniture, as in the panels of the arms on the chair of Sitamun, (page 17), Bes was a household god who was often depicted as a lion, as on the jar in the form of a standing lion (page 81). He was also a protective deity, and in this role he would safeguard the deceased against enemies with a ferocious growl like that indicated on his green-stained ivory face. The inner side of this curved part is also darkly stained, and an upside-down lotus plant is engraved on its surface. While usually shown without any cushion to soften the hard surface on which the head lies, some headrests have been found that still have soft cloth wrapped around them.

Case for a Mirror

ORIGINALLY THE CASE CONTAINED A MIRROR, but when Carter examined the large cartouche-shaped chest placed in the Treasury, he found that the thieves had already stolen the mirror. He suggested, therefore, that it was probably made of a precious material. The case consists of two parts, both of which were made of wood overlaid in sheet gold. Thin sheets of silver lined the interior, and the same metal was used for the knobs by which the case was sealed. Colored glass is used for the majority of the inlays on the lid, but carnelian and quartz were utilized as well.

An inscription with Tutankhamun's names, epithets, and relationship to specific gods is written around the loop of the upper sections of both parts of the box and also in a column in the vertical part. Within the loop of the lower part of the case are two cartouches, each with a uraeus at its side. The cartouches, which contain the throne and personal names of the king, and the serpents, are surmounted by solar disks. The corresponding area on the lid has the throne name of the king written with a winged beetle in place of the traditional one. It is flanked by two serpents whose heads are surmounted by solar disks and whose tails terminate in the hieroglyphic sign for "infinity" (shen). Below the name is a lotus, and the entire composition, inlaid in glass and semiprecious stones, was probably meant to be a reference to a myth involving the birth of the sun god (page 29).

The shape of the case takes the form of the hieroglyph ankh which can mean not only "life," but also "mirror." Such a use illustrates the adaptability and versatility of the writing system of ancient Egypt.

Pair of Earrings

ALTHOUGH THIEVES HAD STOLEN the majority of jewelry from the tomb shortly after Tutankhamun's death, several pieces, in addition to those on the mummy, survived into modern times. The large cartouche-shaped box in the Treasury contained a few such objects, including this elaborate pair of earrings.

The practice of men wearing this type of jewelry seems to be indicated at least as early as the reign of Amenhotep III, when statues have pierced earlobes but their use may have occurred earlier, since the mummy of his father, Thutmosis IV, apparently had pierced ears. It was commonplace during the Amarna period for men to wear earrings, and the representations of Tutankhamun almost always depict him with pierced ears, as in the golden mask. In one representation of him, where Tutankhamun is shown on the lotus, the king still has the back of a metal earring in his left ear.

The pendant of the earring consists of a bird whose golden outstretched wings are inlaid with colored glass, faience, calcite, and quartz. The head is fashioned of a translucent blue glass. Compare the opaque glass in the headrest (page 93). In each talon is the hieroglyph *shen*, meaning "infinity." The flexible suspension, composed of inlaid gold, ends in five hooded cobras.

The horizontal earpiece terminates with a button on either end, and two serpents flank the button that would be on the outer surface of the ear. Composed of a circular inlay of either clear glass or quartz crystal, this button has a portrait of the king fashioned on its underside. When worn—and there is some indication of wear on the post—a portrait in profile of Tutankhamun wearing a blue crown faced the living king.

Floral Collar of Faience Beads

THIS COLLAR CONSISTS OF SEVERAL ROWS of faience beads. While the technique of making faience had been in existence long before Tutankhamun came to the throne, it was only in the reign of his predecessor, Akhenaten, that these brightly colored collars imitating floral garlands first came into extensive use. Each row represents a particular fruit or berry, a petal, or a leaf.

Cornflower, lotus, and mandrake were among the flowers, and olive and willow were the trees whose leaves the Egyptians of the New Kingdom regularly used for their garlands. The berries were usually from the nightshade plant. P. E. Newberry, one of Carter's associates, was able to determine the season in which Tutankhamun was buried based on the growing seasons of the plants used in the king's garlands. According to Newberry, the burial occurred from the middle of March to the end of April. One of the many garlands placed around the third, or innermost, coffin (page 151), consisted of both real flowers and glass beads. Other collars made completely of faience beads were found on the mummy, and still others were strewn about the various chambers of the tomb.

Made of ground quartzite combined with an element for pigmentation, the faience beads could be shaped by hand or cast in a mold. They were then dried and fired, producing a hard, porcelainlike finish. The white glaze of the terminals illustrated here contains an elaborate design consisting of several rows of floral petals, flowers, and fruit. Five flexible strands of beads, each ending in a blossom, are suspended from the terminals.

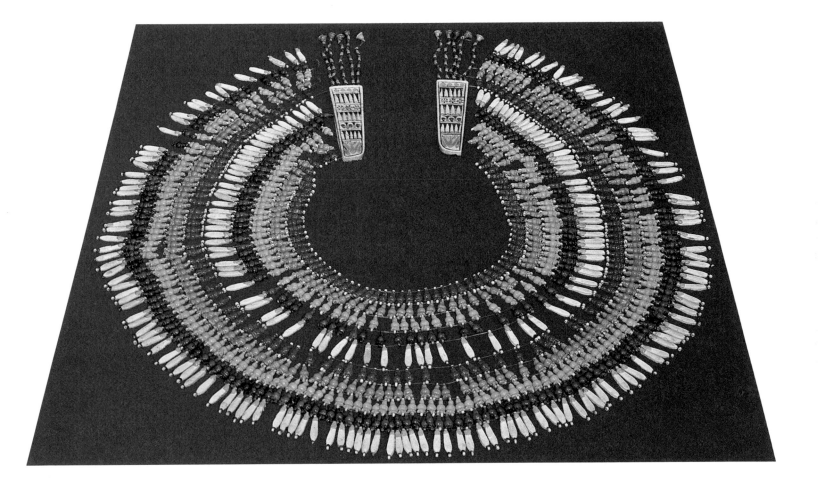

Flexible Collar
in the Form of a Vulture

AFTER HE UNWRAPPED EIGHT LAYERS of the linen that surrounded the mummy, Carter came across several collars, the most elaborate of which represented a vulture, whose wings were composed of two hundred and fifty individual golden plaques. The vulture goddess, Nekhbet, was placed across the chest of Tut. Her upwardly curving wings were draped over his shoulders, and the counterweight, attached to the collar by means of a gold wire, was suspended down his back. Almost the entire piece, except parts of the head and feet, contain inlays that are set with pieces of glass in a variety of colors that imitate semiprecious stones such as carnelian, jasper, turquoise, and lapis lazuli. However, the beak and eye are made of obsidian— a volcanic glass. The reverse side is also finished, and each segment of the wing is engraved in a feather pattern. Further engraving is visible on the upper part of the legs, but the *shen* hieroglyphs, grasped by Nekhbet's claws, are inlaid with red and blue glass.

The advances in the techniques of making glass that occurred during the New Kingdom were responsible for the increased use and elaboration of inlays. Heretofore, such intricacy of design was difficult to produce, since the semiprecious stones were quite hard, and there was a great risk of shattering during the cutting if the pieces needed for the inlays were very small. Moreover, the necessary colors were now readily available, since the glass could be produced locally. In contrast, the stones had to be mined or quarried, and, in some cases, imported from foreign countries.

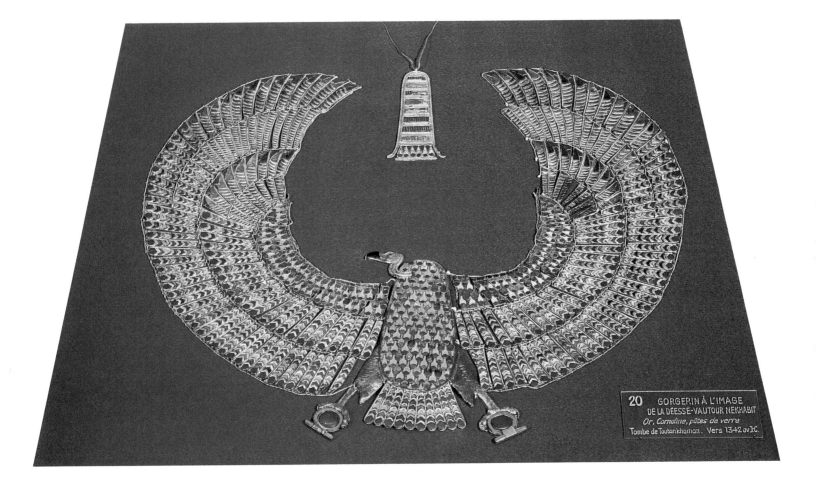

Necklace with Pendant
in the Form of a Vulture

NEKHBET (PAGE 103) IS THE INSPIRATION for another piece of Tutankhamun's jewelry. It was probably used during the lifetime of the king, since it was so close to his mummy, having been placed between the eleventh and twelfth layers of wrapping. Carter found it encircling the neck and extending down over the chest of the king. Many of the more than one hundred and forty pieces of jewelry found on the mummy were ceremonial, amuletic, or ritual. They were produced for the Afterlife. Others, however, were from the king's personal collection, and these were placed among the innermost wrappings.

Nekhbet, the protective deity of Upper Egypt, was part of the king's titulary, along with her Lower Egyptian counterpart, the cobra goddess, Wadjet. Here, the pendant, depicting her in the form of the vulture, is fashioned of solid gold. The surface is covered, except for the lapis lazuli beak and obsidian eye, with colored glass. According to Egyptologist Cyril Aldred, it may be the earliest example of enameling. Unlike glass inlays, which were cut to fit like stones, these were apparently introduced in powdered form and then melted in place. The precision of the jeweler's craft in ancient Egypt is also seen in the detailed engraving on the head, which was cast separately and then gold-soldered to the body. Moreover, the entire reverse side of the vulture is engraved in a feather pattern, and a carved pendant with the king's throne name is suspended around its neck.

The alternating gold and lapis lazuli links of the chain are inlaid with circles of colored glass and bordered with tiny gold and blue glass beads. The clasp takes the form of falcons depicted in an attitude of sleep or rest. Unlike the pendant, it is inlaid mainly with semiprecious stones.

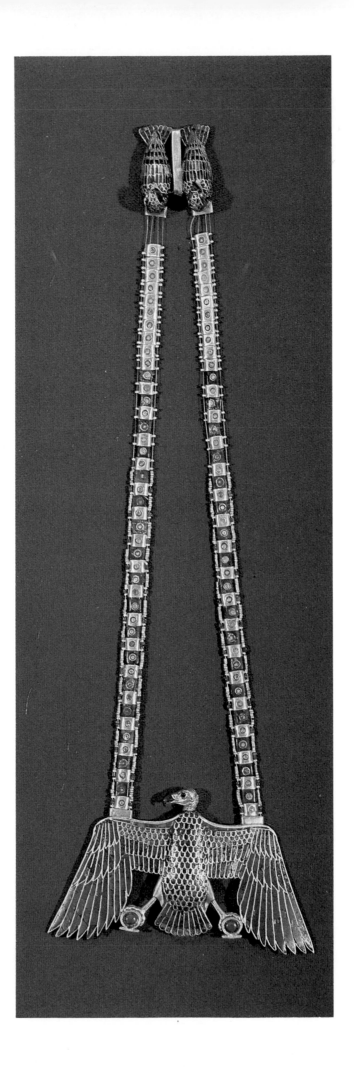

Shrine-Shaped Pendant

THIS PENDANT, ALONG WITH SEVEN OTHERS, was carefully wrapped in linen and placed in a compartment of the gilded base of the god Anubis in the Treasury (page 117). Much of the contents of the chest were stolen, and the original wrapping and seals on this jewelry was disturbed. Its architectonic design is reminiscent of a shrine or a pylon (gateway to a temple), a shape that was used frequently in Egyptian jewelry. There is an inlaid cavetto cornice, below which is a border of stylized flowers. The sides, retaining the same hues of polychrome glass, are composed of bands of alternating size and color. Within the shrine is a vulture, and it, along with the accompanying inscription, is fashioned in a carefully wrought openwork design.

Although the vulture is similar in design and composition to those on other pieces of jewelry (page 105), it does not represent the goddess Nekhbet. According to the inscription above the bird's head, the vulture is the celestial goddess, Nut. Like Nekhbet, her wings are spread out while she grasps the hieroglyph for "infinity" *(shen)* in her talons. Nut as a vulture appears on the ceiling of one of the shrines in which Tutankhamun's coffin was placed. It was Nut who would spread out her wings to protect the king forever.

The throne name of the king, Nebkheperura, written in reverse in the cartouche, follows Tutankhamun's designation as the "Son of Ra." Behind the vulture's head is another cartouche, and here his personal name, Tutankhamun, is in reverse, and the following epithet, which should be "Ruler of the Southern Heliopolis," omits the word for "ruler." Instead of the usual designation, "The good god, Lord of the two Lands," he is called "The good ruler." This reference is not common for Tutankhamun, but it was a phrase frequently used to describe Akhenaton. The pendant was attached to its necklace by means of holes in the short golden pieces on the top.

Pendant with Udjat Eye

LYING OVER THE CHEST OF THE MUMMIFIED BODY of Tutankhamun, this necklace and pendant, along with two other pectorals, were placed between the twelfth and thirteenth layers of bandages. Showing signs of wear, they were probably from the king's personal collection of jewelry. The necklace has three strands of blue, red, and green faience beads and gold spacers. The counterweight, not visible here, consists of three hieroglyphs attached to a gold bar; the outer ones are *djed*, a symbol of Osiris, and the central one is *tyet*, a symbol of Isis.

On the right side of the pectoral is Wadjet, the cobra goddess of Lower Egypt, wearing the red crown symbolic of the northern part of the kingdom. The protective goddess of Upper Egypt, Nekhbet, wears an *atef* crown rather than the tall white crown that is traditionally associated with her. In her talons is the *shen* hieroglyph.

The central element is the udjat eye, a composite form uniting the human eye and eyebrow with the markings below the eye of a falcon. Like the rest of the piece, the inlays are of colored glass and some stone set in gold.

The eye was traditionally associated with the god Horus, with whom the living king was identified. In Egyptian mythology Seth, who murdered his brother Osiris, battles against his avenging son Horus. In the fray Horus's eye is torn out and damaged. Restored and returned to its owner by the god Thoth, the eye is presented by Horus to his father to revivify him. The eye became a popular amulet and, as a hieroglyph, it meant "sound" or "healthy."

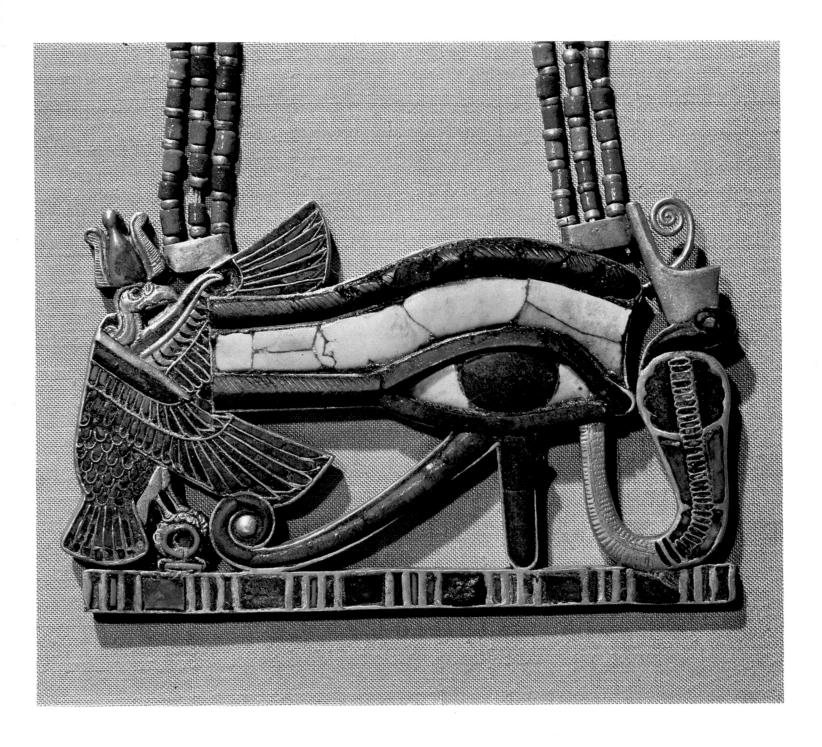

Necklace with Pendant Depicting
the Solar Beetle Flanked by Baboons

LIKE MANY OF THE ITEMS in Tutankhamun's tomb, this intricately designed necklace and pendant reflects aspects of the traditional religion that the young king restored. It was found in a box in the Treasury with other similar objects, probably all of which were originally from the king's personal collection of jewelry. The central motif depicts the rising of the sun. The scarab beetle, who sustains its young from the ball of dung it carries, was associated in Egyptian mythology with the sun, as the means by which it crosses the heaven every day. Here, the golden beetle, inlaid with lapis lazuli, is in the bark of the sun, holding the solar disk in its front legs and the *shen* hieroglyph ("infinity") in its hind legs. The hieroglyph *pet* ("sky") above is fashioned of lapis lazuli and inlaid with fourteen golden stars; the water below is lapis lazuli inlaid with golden waves. On either side is the hieroglyph *was* ("dominion"). The scarab is accompanied by two baboons, animals frequently associated with the rising sun. Moreover, the god Thoth, who is often represented in the form of a baboon, usually accompanies the sun in the bark. Upon the baboons' heads are the lunar disk and crescent. The two are seated on the roof of a golden shrine (page 55), worshipping the sun as it rises.

The openwork of the pendant is repeated in the links of the chain, each of which is bordered on both sides by gold and lapis lazuli beads. The majority of the design of the plaques forms a hieroglyphic message containing a central sign—"endurance" *(djed)*, "life" *(ankh)*, or "protection" *(sa)*. Each is flanked by the hieroglyph for "dominion" *(was)*; the *heb* basket, apparently here meaning "every," is underneath. Only the two links closest to the pendant differ. One contains the dual thrones of the jubilee, while the other has the god Heh holding signs for years, each of which rests on a tadpole.

The clasp, which functions also as a counterweight, depicts, Heh in an architectonic setting. Holding the sign for "infinity" *(shen)* above his head, he is flanked by cobras wearing the crowns of Upper and Lower Egypt.

110

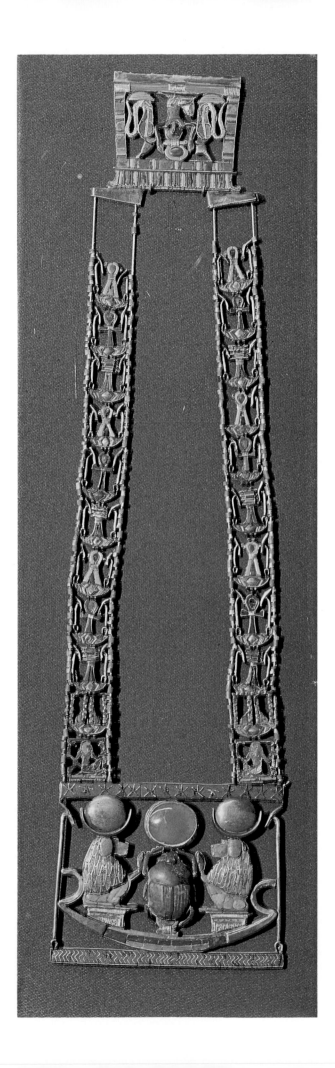

Pendant with Symbols
of the Sun and Moon

TUTANKHAMUN WAS THE CENTRAL FIGURE in the counterreformation, and, although most of the objects in his tomb reflect either directly or indirectly the traditional religion, few pieces have as many motifs utilized in one composition as does this pendant found in the Treasury. Its original necklace was a simple linen cord.

The central element in the elaborate openwork pectoral is a winged scarab. Its body is carved chalcedony, a green semiprecious stone, which here is set in gold. The inlaid forelegs are those of a beetle, while the wings, tail, and hind legs are those of a falcon; the figure thus combines parts of two solar deities, the falcon and scarab, into one unified creature. The incised gold talons grasp inlaid *shen* hieroglyphs and plants symbolic of Upper and Lower Egypt, lotuses and a lily. A cobra wearing a disk of the sun, another solar emblem, is on either side of the winged scarab. Below is a row of inlaid colored circles to which is attached a border of flowers separated by round inlays of colored glass with gold circles in their centers.

The golden bark with papyriform ends has a central section inlaid with turquoise. Inside the boat at each end is a serpent wearing a solar disk. In the center is the sacred eye (page 109), which is often associated with the moon. Attached to the eyebrow is the golden crescent and silver disk of the moon. On its surface are three golden figures, the central one of which is the king. On his left is the ibis-headed god, Thoth, who also has lunar associations. Both have a crescent and disk of the moon on their heads. Before them stands Ra-Horakhty, a solar deity, who wears the disk of the sun and a uraeus. The pectoral, therefore, depicts a multitude of solar and lunar symbols and deities.

Bezel of a Ring

THE SHANK OF THIS RING has long since disappeared, but its bezel—the part of a ring where gems can be attached—along with seven other rings found wrapped in a scarf and stuffed into a box, are part of the interesting mystery that Howard Carter solved. The rings, probably originally from the Treasury, were placed in the box in the Antechamber by the necropolis officials who restored order to the tomb. The presence of the royal scarf presented a problem, however, since it, like the rings, was not among the original contents of the box in which it was placed by the officials. Moreover, it hardly seemed worthy of the theft, considering the other, more valuable objects in the tomb. Carter concluded that the thieves wrapped up the small items in the scarf in an attempt to carry out as many objects as possible. The presence of both the scarf and the rings may indicate that the robbers were caught in the act, or that they left their plunder in their hurried exit.

The top of the ring depicts a very detailed scene containing many of the traditional gods of Egypt. The tallest figure (on the right) is that of Ra-Horakhty seated on a throne. He is worshipped by three figures; the central one is the king, and the remaining two are baboons wearing a lunar disk and crescent (page 111). The deities Nekhbet (on the right) and Horus (on the left), extend their protective wings around the entire group.

Approximately one inch across and one-half inch deep, this miniature sculpture was cast in solid gold. It displayed the most elaborate decorations of any of the rings found in the tomb.

Anubis

THIS RECUMBENT FIGURE OF A JACKAL represents the god Anubis. Slightly more than three feet long, it crouched protectively near the entrance to the Treasury. Carved of wood that has been covered with a black resin, the life-size statue has gilded ears, collar, and scarf. His nails are made of silver, the eyebrow and cosmetic line are gilded metal, and the eye is calcite and obsidian. The base upon which he rests, composed of carved and gilded wood, takes the shape of a shrine. Each side contains a central pattern bordered on three sides by an inscription. Symbols of the gods Isis and Osiris occur in some of the panels. The shrine is actually a compartmentalized chest which contained among other things, eight large pendants (page 107). Under the base was a sledge with four carrying poles.

The statue was originally covered with a thin shawl and scarf, and around his neck was a floral garland. Over the figure was fringed linen that bore an inscription dated the seventh year of Akhenaton's reign.

Anubis was the god of embalming, and, although in the earliest times he was the primary god of the Underworld, he is eventually replaced in that role by Osiris. At the judgment of the dead, Anubis is the "master of the balance," the scale which weighs the heart of the deceased against the feather of Maat. If the pans do not tilt, the deceased would be brought before the god of the Underworld, Osiris, having been judged "true of voice." The hearts of those who did not pass the test were devoured by a mythical beast.

Statuette of the God Ihy

AMONG THE MANY REPRESENTATIONS of the traditional gods of the Egyptian pantheon that were in the Treasury, there were two of the god Ihy. One of the few deities to be shown without clothes, Ihy is the son of the goddess Hathor. Made of wood covered with a dark resin, the figure holds a gilded sistrum in his right hand. His eyebrows have been gilded, and the whites and pupils of his eyes are indicated. He is depicted with the sidelock of youth, the traditional coiffure for this young god (page 89). The coloration, symbolizing the fertile soil, may indicate his association with rebirth.

While Ihy is often referred to in the literature as the god of music, his role here is clearly funerary. He is a friendly god, one who will protect the deceased against any of the demons or evil deities who might act against him. In the Coffin Texts (a body of funerary spells, recorded on the inner walls of coffins, which formed the basis of the Book of the Dead), Ihy is referred to as one of the manifestations of the deceased (Spell 334)—one of the gods into which the dead person is transformed. Tutankhamun would also travel with Ihy across the horizon. Ihy is a sky god because his mother was Hathor, a goddess who had celestial associations. He is also one of the divinities addressed by the deceased when pronouncing the "negative confession" (Chapter 125 of the Book of the Dead). If he were judged acceptable, he would then enter into the Afterlife.

Gilded Wooden Head of a Cow

THIS WOODEN CARVING of the head and neck of a cow found in the Treasury in front of the canopic chest (page 93) was covered with a thin layer of gesso. The head and part of the neck were then gilded, while the lower portion of the neck and the pedestal base were coated with a dark resin. The horns, which received the same varnish, consist of gessoed wood covered with a thin metal sheet of either copper or bronze. Inlays of glass and stone form the different parts of the eye.

The goddess Hathor was often represented in the form of a cow, and, as such, was depicted on the walls of many Theban tombs dating to the New Kingdom. When portrayed in the papyrus marsh, her body is usually obscured, hidden by the thicket and the western mountain. Only her head is visible, and it is perhaps this aspect of her that is rendered here in three dimensions. Hathor was known as the mistress of the western desert, where the necropolis was located, and would, therefore, be of assistance to the deceased. She is frequently referred to in the Coffin Texts and the Book of the Dead. It is to her that the deceased comes upon entering the Afterlife, and it is she who will anoint him and give him life among the dead.

Part of the Funerary Bed
in the Form of a Cow

WHEN CARTER'S TEAM HAD CLEARED the entrance corridor of its debris, they stood before the sealed doorway to the first room (later called the Antechamber) of the tomb of Tutankhamun. Carter poked a hole through the three-thousand-year-old plaster and extended a candle into the blackness to test for noxious gases. When he peered in, his eyes took a few moments to adjust to the darkness; eventually, he saw the outlines of objects and "everywhere, the glint of gold." Directly opposite the door was this funerary bed. It was the central one of three couches in animal form, each of which is made of gessoed wood, covered in gold. In front was the lion bed, while behind was a bed composed of elements of a hippopotamus, a crocodile, and a leopard.

Colored glass inlays form parts of the eye and the spots on the skin. The head is rendered realistically, while the side and legs, conforming to the shape of the couch, are attenuated. Made of several independent parts, the bed was prepared most likely for funerary purposes only and set up in place in the tomb. The metal attachment holding the animal in place still remains intact.

The symbolism evoked by the form of the couch is complicated and encompasses the roles of several traditional deities. The cow may represent the goddess Hathor (page 121) who is responsible for the resurrection of the deceased. The cow with a solar disk between the horns is a form often associated with the goddess Mehetweret, a celestial deity who plays an important part in the birth of the sun god, whose disk she bears. It is from her, the nocturnal sky, that the sun god is born each day. The sky goddess, Nut, is also represented in bovine form, and the sun god is pictured sailing across her back. An inscription on part of the frame, however, refers to a deity in the form of a lion. The identification may be an error, for the corresponding inscription on the lion bed refers to Mehetweret. In all likelihood the funerary couch in the form of a cow represented a conflation of the attributes of all these cow goddesses. They were to ensure the ascension of Tutankhamun to the next world.

Wooden Statuette of the King
Upon a Funerary Bed

THIS MINIATURE WOODEN VERSION of the innermost burial equipment of Tutankhamun had its own outer wooden coffin. Although placed in the Treasury, it resembles the mummy of the king and the carved wooden funerary couch in the shape of a lion that supported his three outer coffins in the Burial Chamber. The horizontal and vertical inscriptions on the figure are representative of the golden bands around the mummy; they invoke the goddess Nut and refer to the king as revered before several gods. The hieroglyphs carved between the legs of the couch give the titles and name of the official Maya who, it is recorded, made the statuette for his lord, Tutankhamun. In addition, Maya, who also dedicated a shawabty figure (page 131), may have taken a prominent role in the building of the tomb, since he holds the title "Superintendent of Building-Works in the Necropolis."

Although model tools like those found with shawabty figures accompanied the statuette, it is unlikely that this object, which has no parallels, served the same purpose. The birds at each elbow, although not quite freestanding, are almost completely carved away from the single block of wood from which the piece is fashioned. One of the birds has the head of a human, and such a figure is a traditional representation of an element of the personality called a *ba* (sometimes referred to as a soul). The other appears to be a falcon and may, according to the funerary literature, represent one of the manifestations of the deceased. It is possible, however, that it too is an element of the personality. The kings of ancient Egypt were identified with the falcon god Horus; they were his living embodiment. The figure of the falcon here may depict the *ba* or the *ka* of Horus, thereby portraying the divine nature of the pharaoh. The two birds, one human, one divine, would then be a concrete representation of the two aspects that constitute kingship in ancient Egypt.

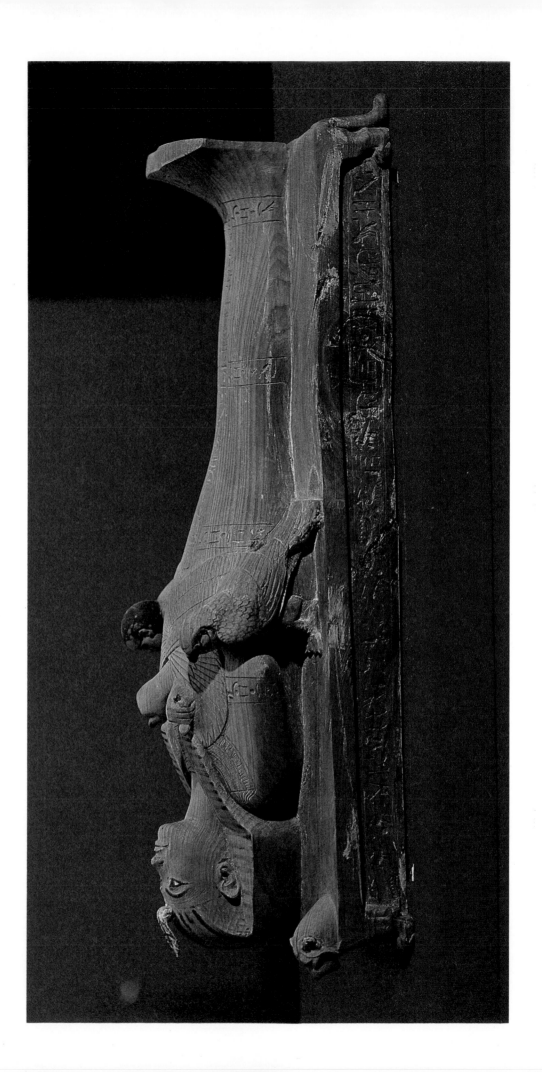

Painted Wooden Torso
of the King

THIS CARVED WOODEN STATUE, smoothed with gesso and then painted, is a life-size representation of the king. Carter recorded that the figure was beneath one of the large ceremonial chariots in the southern end of the Antechamber. The arms have intentionally been severed below the bicep, and the body extends to just below the hips. Tutankhamun wears a simple white garment and a flat-topped crown with protecting uraeus, similar to a crown that Nefertiti often uses (page 21). His ears are pierced, and his skin is painted a reddish brown in the convention typical for representing males.

Although Carter had suggested that the figure may have been a mannequin, similar to a clothes-dummy, which would hold the garments and jewelry of the king, it is difficult to find parallel pieces. Other scholars have pointed out that this torso and several statues from the Middle Kingdom, which are somewhat similar in appearance, may all be related to the rebirth or resurrection of the king in association with his identification with the god Osiris. In tombs of the Old Kingdom, there are also busts similar to this one. They are heads or torsos sculpted to look as if they were emerging from the floor or the wall. They appear to be images of the *ka* (the corporeal twin and essential nature of the deceased) coming up from the burial chamber and entering the offering chapel through or near the false door, the place where offerings to the deceased could be made. Because of these parallels it is likely that this enigmatic statue has a funerary, rather than domestic purpose.

Painted Scene from the Tomb of Tutankhamun

TUTANKHAMUN, ACCOMPANIED by his corporeal twin the *ka*, embraces the lord of the West, Osiris. His face is painted green, symbolizing vegetation. His white garments are the wrappings and shrouds of linen that also cover the mummy. On the eastern end of this wall (page 27), Tutankhamun, already deceased, appears in the form of Osiris.

Painted on the west (left) end of the north wall of the Burial Chamber, this scene is complemented by two others. The east part (right) portrays the god's father, Aye, engaged in the ritual of "Opening the Mouth" of the mummiform Tutankhamun (page 27). In the center of the wall Tutankhamun stands before the celestial goddess Nut (page 149).

The westernmost group, pictured here, shows, on the right, the *ka* of the king holding an *ankh* ("life") in his left hand. The inscription refers to the figure as the "Ka of the King, Foremost of the Palace." Directly above his head is the hieroglyphic sign for *ka*, the upraised arms. Inside the arms, the falcon god Horus perches atop a rectangular structure representing the palace; a hooded cobra, the uraeus, is before him. The hieroglyphs written within the structure mean "Strong Bull," and the entire composition resting on the hieroglyph *ka* is the Horus name (sometimes also referred to as a *ka* name) of Tutankhamun, one of the several names that make up the titulary of the king. In death, the king (center) becomes identified with Osiris (left). His *ka*, an invisible manifestation of his being in life, survives in the next world, and it is to the *ka* that offerings are to be made.

Shawabty Statuettes
of the King

THESE THREE MINIATURE FIGURES of Tutankhamun in the form of Osiris are made of wood, while parts of the headdress, the flail, the collar, and the arm bands (in two instances) have been gilded. Shawabty figures first appear early in the Middle Kingdom (c. 2100 B.C.) as substitutes for the mummy. Their name may derive from the material out of which some of them were carved—*sheweb* ("persea wood"). By the end of the Middle Kingdom they were believed to perform the required agricultural activities of the deceased in the Afterlife.

With the advent of the New Kingdom (c. 1575 B.C.) the figures begin to have religious inscriptions carved on them. Although the facial features are usually generalized, the owner is identified by the indication of his name somewhere on the figure. Covering the lower part of the body is a version of the funerary spell, Chapter 6 of the Book of the Dead. The shawabty statuettes of Tutankhamun are no exception to the rule, and they are instructed to perform the labor for their masters when the call is made. In tombs of private people there were often three hundred and sixty-five shawabty, one for each day of the year, and, in addition, a group usually numbering around forty acted as foremen. The three figures shown here number among the over four hundred that Carter recorded in the Treasury. The Annex contained several hundred more, and one was found even in the Antechamber. In total, more than seven hundred were placed in the tomb.

Six of the shawabty were dedicated by two of Tutankhamun's faithful subjects. Like the statuette of the king on a funerary bed (page 125), Maya made one of the shawabty for his king. The figure on the left, wearing the blue crown, was among the five shawabty that were presented by the General of the Army, Minnakht. Almost all of the shawabty figures in the tomb show some facial resemblance to the king, and this may have been because of a special royal command.

Gilded Wooden Statuettes
of the King

THE TREASURY CONTAINED THIRTY-TWO STATUETTES like these packed in twenty-two wooden boxes stored together along the southern wall of the chamber. Each figure stood on a darkly varnished pedestal, and linen, which can be dated to the reign of Akhenaton because of ink labels, enveloped the statuette, except for the face. Floral garlands were draped over a few of the images, and all but one of the chests retained the original seals. Twenty-seven represented deities, and five portrayed the king; all of them received a smooth coating of gesso before being gilded. The eyes contain inlays of glass, and the items the king holds, his sandals, and the serpent at his brow are made of gilded bronze.

In the foreground, Tutankhamun, holding staves of his office, wears the tall white crown of Upper Egypt. To the left is another similar image; this one, however, has the red crown of Lower Egypt. In the background, the goddess Menkeret carries Tutankhamun, who wears a close-fitting garment and the crown of Lower Egypt. Behind the goddess is the king as harpooner (page 43) and behind that figure is Tutankhamun upon the black leopard. All of the statuettes are rendered in the naturalistic style introduced during the Amarna period, but it is the pantheon of traditional gods that is represented, not the Aton, the god of Akhenaton.

Seated Statuette
of Leonine Goddess

AMONG THE TRADITIONAL DEITIES restored during the reign of Tutankhamun was the goddess Sekhmet. This figure was among the twenty-seven that were stored in several boxes in the Treasury. Carved of wood, they were covered with gesso, smoothed, and gilded. The eyes and noses have inlays of colored glass. The goddess has the body of a human female, but the head of a lioness. She wears a wig commonly used during the New Kingdom, and there is a solar disk atop her head. The pattern of her floral collar (page 101) is visible only between the frontal part of her wig; the straps of her empire-waist gown are indicated just below the collar. The garment she wears represents the classic dress with applied beaded netting. The throne on which she sits is typical for both royal and divine figures (page 39) of the New Kingdom. The plants symbolic of Upper and Lower Egypt (pages 61 and 79) are in relief on a panel on the side, and the whole is covered in a feather pattern.

Sekhmet, whose name means "Powerful One," was primarily regarded as a war goddess. In a funerary text, she is the protectress of several groups of foreigners. The Memphite triad of which she was part included the gods Ptah and Nefertem; they are also represented in the tomb. Along with her husband, Ptah, she destroyed enemies of the sun god and of the king who accompanied him.

Statue of Netcherankh

THIS FIGURE OF A DEITY was among the thirty-two statues stored in the twenty-two darkly varnished shrine-shaped chests in the Treasury. Although it appears to be the uraeus that frequently is part of Egyptian iconography, there is an identification on the base that labels the serpent Netcherankh, the "living god." Like the painted yellow inscriptions on the pedestal of the other statues, Tutankhamun is referred to as "beloved of the god." Despite the presence of the name of the deity, its function is not well known. The same term, "living god," occurs in the Coffin Texts referring to the deceased. Later texts, however, refer to serpent deities who aid the deceased in his travels during certain of the twelve hours of the night. An emblem carved on the neck of the creature is usually associated with the goddess Neith (page 99), and she too figures in this voyage.

   The serpent is made of gilded wood, and the base, also of wood, has a dark varnish coating. Although the markings on the back and hood are somewhat stylized, there is a certain degree of realism, except for the shortness of the tail. The eyes, made of quartz crystal or clear glass, are painted on the underside and are set in metal sockets.

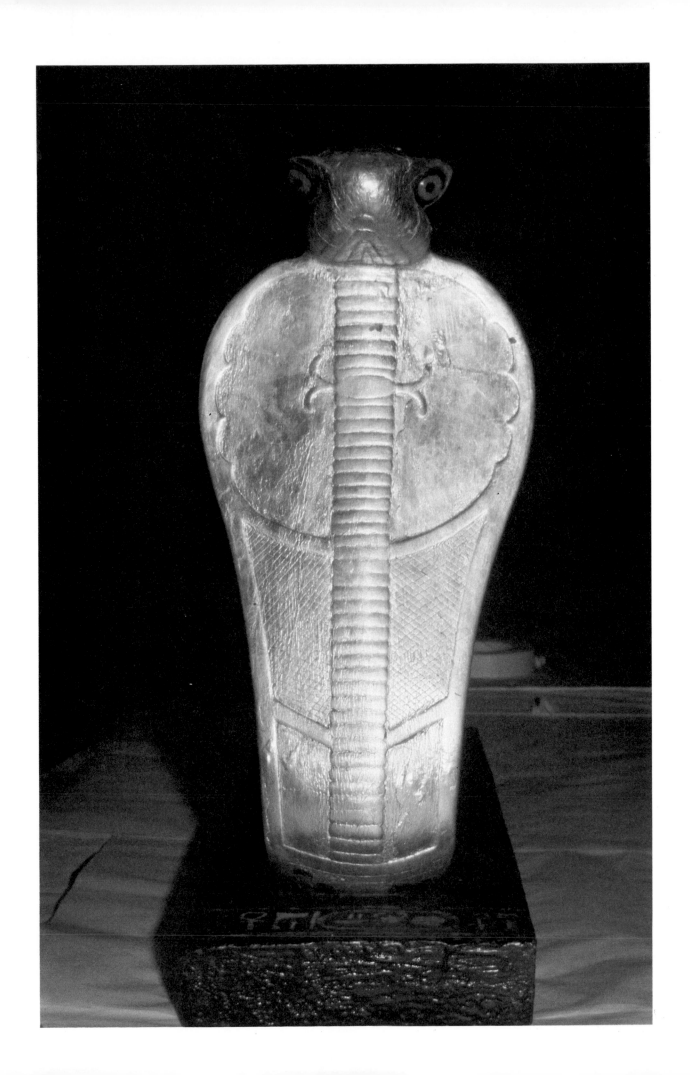

Canopic Chest of Gilded Wood

MUCH OF THE TREASURY contained objects that would serve to aid the king in his rebirth. One of the most important of these was the canopic chest, for inside, carefully protected, were the internal organs of Tutankhamun. The four most important organs—the lungs, liver, stomach, and intestines—were removed from the body through an incision usually made on the left side of the body during the process of mummification. They were each treated and then stored separately. The heart, in most cases, was left in the body.

In the case of Tutankhamun, these organs were housed in a very elaborate outer structure, made of wood covered in gesso and gilded. It rests on a sledge and the outer canopy consists of four supports and a cavetto cornice with a frieze of hooded cobras with solar disks. The same motif is repeated on the upper part of the shrine itself.

A beautifully carved goddess was positioned at each side. With elongated outstretched arms in a gesture of protection, each goddess was responsible for a particular organ. In the foreground, Isis guarded the liver, while to the right, Selket watched over the intestines. Not visible here is the protectress of the stomach, Neith, or of the lungs, Nepthys.

The three-dimensional representations of the goddesses represent a departure from the traditional attitude of figures. Each figure glances off to the side—a strong contrast to the frontality of other Egyptian statues. It is likely that the environment influenced the composition, but it is also possible that the naturalistic style of the Amarna period exerted a strong influence.

Selket

ONE OF THE FOUR PROTECTIVE GODDESSES who stand at the sides of the canopic chest (page 139), Selket, like her companions Isis, Nepthys, and Neith, is made of carved wood coated with gesso and gilt. She was fitted into a slot on the sledge by means of a support below her feet. The only paint is that used to delineate her eyes and eyebrows. Upon her head is her emblem, the scorpion, whose sting she was reputed to be able to cure.

In the Coffin Texts, Selket functions as a protectress of the canopic equipment and also as a guardian of the coffin. Her magic is referred to in religious texts, and it was she who would go against the evil serpent Apophis, the enemy of the sun god. Her role was later expanded to that of a protectress of the dead and her varied functions even included aiding during childbirth. She is usually depicted as a human female.

In the tomb of Tutankhamun it is Selket who will protect the intestines of the king. Placed in a miniature coffin (page 155), and according to inscriptional evidence, this organ was identified as one of the four sons of Horus, Kebehsenuef. The hieroglyph on the lid of the case states that Selket will put her arms upon what is inside her, an apparent reference to the representation of her on the underside of the lid and the three-dimensional sculpture of her with outstretched arms.

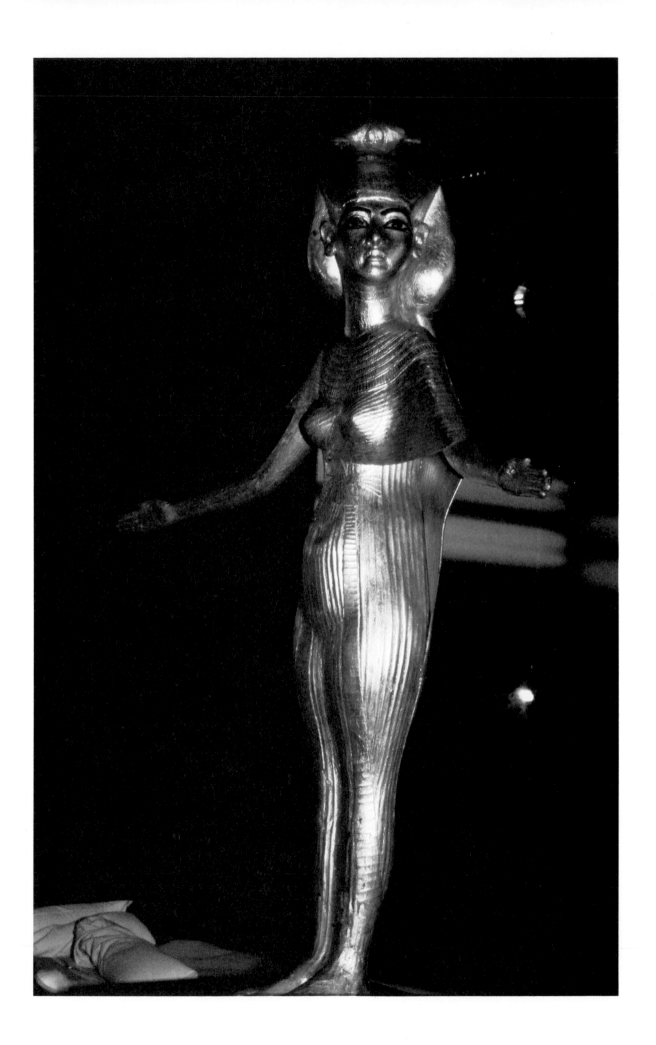

Selket

THIS REPRESENTATION OF SELKET marks a departure from the traditional pose and gesture of Egyptian statuary. She glances off to the side in contrast to the rigid frontality of most figures in Egyptian art. It is likely that the environment for this statue and the three similar ones was partially responsible for this unique attitude. Each goddess, although carved as a completely freestanding piece, was fixed in place as a part of a larger composition. The influence of the Amarna period and the extent of experimentation with postures and gestures (pages 23 and 43) during that time probably had a certain effect upon the sculptors of these figures. The elongation of the arms, neck, and fingers, the slight swelling of the abdomen, and the heaviness of the thighs are features all traceable to Amarna prototypes. The natural and gracefully curved lines of the piece also reflect the best of the art produced during Akhenaton's reign.

Selket's head is covered with a scarf that is pulled behind her head. Over her neck and shoulders is a broad collar, and she wears a tight-fitting garment with half-sleeves. Her shawl clings to her left shoulder, falls loosely down her back, and is tied in a knot above her abdomen. Her feet are bare. Her costume is similar to one often worn by Tutankhamun's wife, Ankhesenamun (pages 35 and 57), whose features may have been the model for Selket.

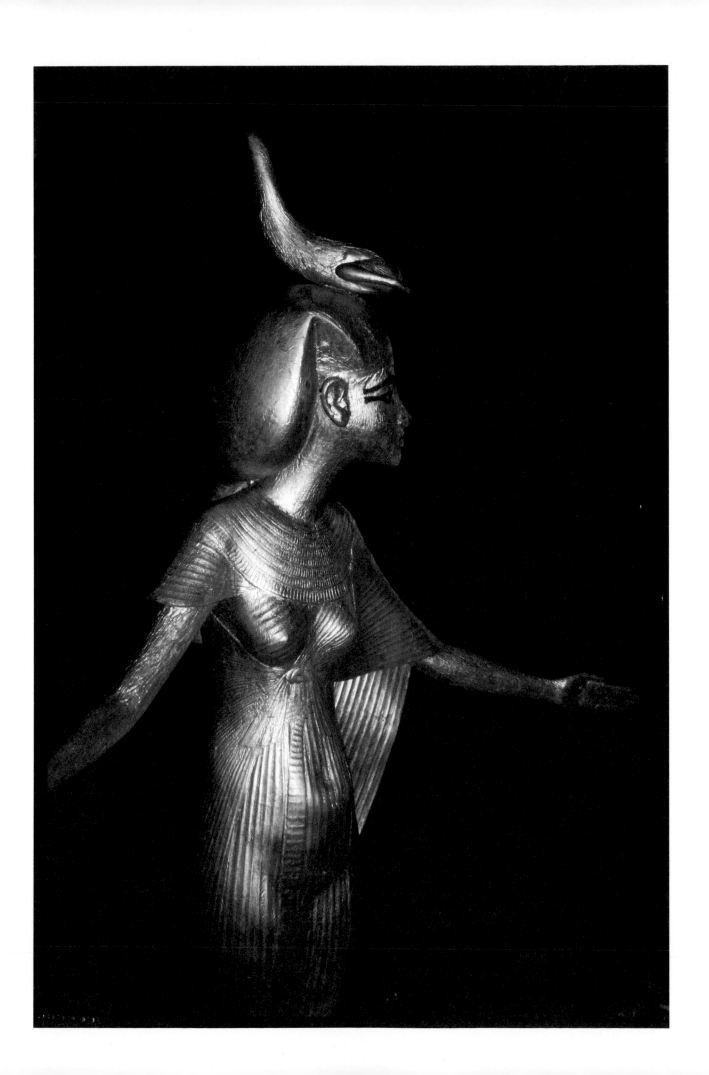

Lid from a Compartment
in the Alabaster Canopic Chest

ONCE CARTER DISMANTLED THE OUTER GILDED WOODEN CHEST (see page 139), another chest, this one of alabaster carved in the shape of a shrine, was revealed. It was covered by a pall of linen. When Carter removed the lid, he found four sculpted heads serving as the lids or stoppers for the four cylindrical compartments into which the interior of the chest was divided.

Each head portrays the features of Tutankhamun, and he wears the *nemes* (or striped) headdress. The protective deities representing Upper and Lower Egypt, Nekhbet and Wadjet, carved as a separate piece, have been inserted just above the brow. The ears of the king are pierced, and many other facial features are indicated or highlighted in either red or black paint. While it appears at first that the artist treated the face somewhat summarily, he did focus on certain details, such as the small red swellings in the corners of the eye (see also page 127), the raised area between the nose and mouth, and the two creases in the neck. The latter feature, when used in conjunction with pierced ears, is an iconographic detail that appears first toward the end of the reign of Amenhotep III. Below the shoulders the piece is recessed so that the stopper would fit into the compartment that had been hollowed out in order to allow the inner case to stand upright.

Life-Size Wooden Statue of the King

PLACED IN THE NORTH END of the Antechamber, this figure of Tutankhamun faced another similar statue, the two acting as guardians before the entrance to the Burial Chamber. Standing approximately five feet six inches tall, the two statues flanked the plastered blind wall behind which lay the mortal remains of the king. The statue is carved in wood, and gilded bronze is the material of the uraeus, sandals, eyebrows, and cosmetic lines. The whites of the eyes are crystalline limestone, and the pupils are obsidian. A black resin covers the exposed parts of the body, while the clothes, jewelry, mace, and staff are gilded over a layer of linen and gesso. A thin shroud of linen originally draped over each figure had all but disintegrated by the time Carter opened the tomb.

The positioning of these statues outside the Burial Chamber may relate to their protective purpose. The inscription on the projecting part of the kilt, however, may indicate another function, since it refers to the statue as the royal *ka* of the sun god, Horakhty. It was this god that the king would accompany in his solar bark, and it was one of the gods with whom he would be identified. As such, the statue could represent one of the aspects of the king. The inscription also calls the king "Osiris," an indication that he is dead and has joined Osiris. This latter association may be the reason for the color of the visible parts of the body. Osiris was frequently shown with black skin to symbolize the fertile land from which all vegetation and, therefore, all life derived. Sometimes illustrated with green skin, the color of vegetation, or perennial life, Osiris symbolized life eternal.

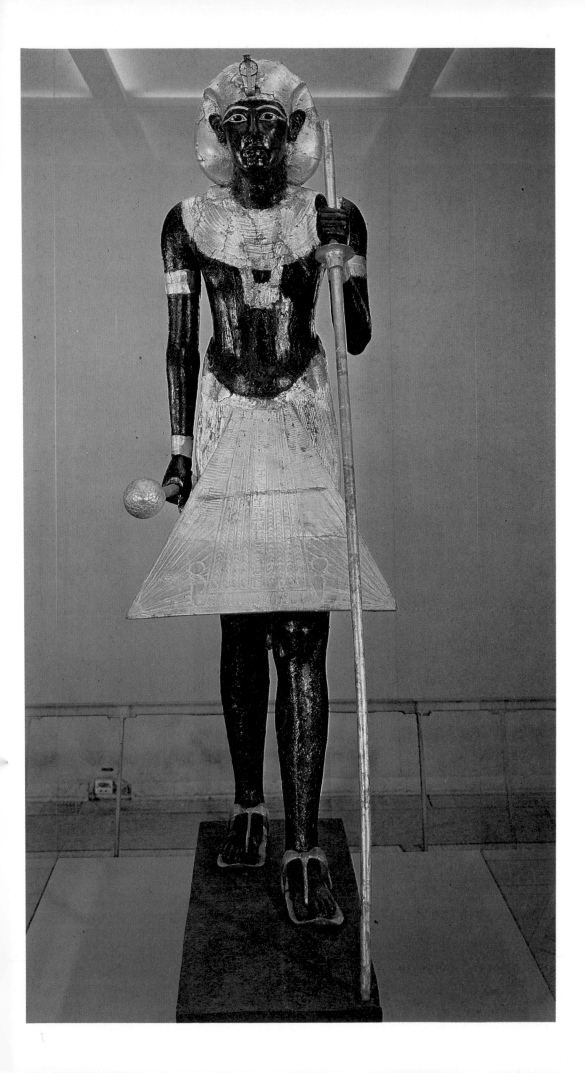

Burial Chamber
of the Tomb of Tutankhamun

TWO GUARDIAN FIGURES of the king (page 149) stood before the entrance to this room, the floor of which was about three feet lower than that of the Antechamber. Upon breaking through the plastered wall to the room, Carter faced what appeared to be a solid wall of gold scarcely two feet from him. This was the gilded wooden outer shrine which almost totally filled the Burial Chamber.

The painted decoration (visible here on the north wall and parts of the east and west walls) on the walls of this room represents the only wall decoration. Vignettes from various funerary texts ordinarily adorned the walls of royal tombs. But only the west wall, depicting several baboons, the solar boat, and demigods, directly relates to a funerary text, illustrating the first of the twelve hours of night. The east wall illustrated the funerary procession led by the courtiers of the king. On the south wall the king was shown in the company of Hathor and Anubis. There is also an inscription, similar to that of Nut on the opposite wall. According to Carter, it is all that remains of the scene with Isis and three gods of the Underworld. It was destroyed in order to remove the shrines and the sarcophagus.

The north wall depicts (left to right) Tutankhamun, together with his *ka*, embracing Osiris (page 129); the king before Nut; and Aye performing the ritual of Opening the Mouth (see page 27). In the central scene, the king, holding a mace, staff, and *ankh*, appears before the celestial goddess Nut. According to the inscription above her head, she will cause health and life to be at the nose of Tutankhamun so that he may live forever.

The surface of the wall has received only a summary treatment, and the painting is not of the best quality. The representations, while traditional in terms of iconography, reflect some of the naturalism and curvilinear style of the Amarna period.

In the foreground, the outermost gilded wooden coffin lies in the carved quartzite sarcophagus. Today, as was true on the day of his entombment, Tutankhamun rests in the Burial Chamber of his tomb in the Valley of the Kings.

Innermost Golden Coffin

LIKE THE INTERNAL ORGANS OF THE KING, his mummy was also within several series of containers. Three mummiform coffins, one inside the other, and weighing over three thousand pounds, were inside a carved quartzite sarcophagus, whose cracked lid was made of granite. The four goddesses, Isis, Selket, Neith, and Nepthys—each carved on a corner—spread protective wings around the sides and utter words on behalf of the deceased king. A wooden canopy with a linen pall with golden rosettes covered the sarcophagus. Four gilt outer shrines, each one adorned with vignettes from funerary texts, were built one over the other; the outermost one of which almost reached the ceiling and was barely two feet from the wall.

When finally extricated from the almost gluelike unguents poured over each coffin, the golden coffin was found to weigh more than two thousand pounds. Slightly more than six feet in length and four feet in width, it is almost one eighth of an inch thick. Lying within the second mummiform coffin, the gold coffin was covered, except for the head, with reddish linen. A stiffened bead and floral collar adorned the neck.

Colored glass, faience, and small pieces of semiprecious stones form the inlays that cover the upper portion of the coffin and include the eyes, eyebrows, and false beard of the king. Strands of gold and faience beads, similar to the gold of honor (page 61), hang around the neck. An inlaid collar is over the upper part of the chest, while two vultures, one with the head of a serpent (page 147), adorn the arms, abdomen, and sides of the figure and parallel the vulture and cobra goddesses upon his brow. A feather pattern and the protective goddesses, Isis and Nepthys, are engraved on the lower part. An inscription in two columns is found on the lower part of the coffin, and Isis, engraved on the foot, spreads out her protective wings and utters the statement, among others, that Tutankhamun will be strong and vigorous and that he will achieve a spiritual state in heaven.

Golden Diadem

In COMPARISON TO THE ORNATENESS of some of the jewelry with which Tutankhamun was buried, this diadem appears almost simple in its decoration. Found between the last few layers of linen bandages, it encircled the head of Tutankhamun's mummy. In design it is similar to a headband often worn by the king (page 55), and its prototypes can be traced back to the ribbons shown on the heads of the figures on the walls of the tombs of the Old Kingdom.

Here, the band, no longer a functional piece of apparel, is interpreted in a permanent material to last an eternity. The decorative circles, held in place by a post with a gold cap, are carnelian; the inlaid borders are blue glass. Following the original model, the band has a knot indicated at the back, and the two ends, hanging close together, fall downward. Two attached streamers flare out on a diagonal, and they are each decorated with cut-out figures of a serpent.

On the front are the protective goddesses of Upper and Lower Egypt, Nekhbet and Wadjet. Their inlays consist of semiprecious stones and colored glass. The hood of the cobra, like that of Necherankh (page 137), has the emblem of the goddess Neith at the neck. Although the vulture and cobra appear to be fixed decorative elements now, Carter did not find them attached to the diadem. Placed along the thighs of the mummy, they have since been applied to the band by means of a sophisticated tongue-and-groove system on the front of the band and the back of the two goddesses.

Miniature Canopic Coffin

EACH OF THE FOUR COMPARTMENTS of the canopic chest held a miniature coffin. Covered in linen, they stood upright in their cylindrical compartments. Each was almost glued to the bottom owing to the hardening of the unguents that had been poured in as part of the ritual. It was the duty of the goddess Nepthys, whose name is inscribed on the front, to protect the lungs of Tutankhamun, which were placed inside, after first being preserved. The figure, fashioned of solid beaten gold, contains inlays of colored glass and semiprecious stones. It is very close in design to the second coffin in which Tutankhamun was buried; in fact, it is almost a miniature version.

The inscription written in the panel on the front are words spoken by the goddess Nepthys. She states that she will protect Hapy; Hapy means the lungs with which the god Hapy is associated. The figure is mummiform, and across the upper part are the protective wings of two vultures, one of which, however, has the head of a cobra. The two represent the goddesses of Upper and Lower Egypt.

The inside of the canopic coffin is completely engraved. The upper part, which corresponds to the lid of the coffin, shows Nepthys with outstretched wings. The remainder of the top and the entire bottom is inscribed with hieroglyphs. The cartouches show indications that the name of Tutankhamun was not original and that it has replaced the name of his elder brother, Smenkhkare. In fact, the face portrayed here is quite distinct from that shown on other pieces.

Golden Mask

WHEN CARTER REMOVED THE LID of the innermost gold coffin, he revealed the mummy of Tutankhamun. Covered with layers of linen bandages and shrouds, among which were placed more than one hundred and forty items of jewelry, the mummy had a golden mask over its head and shoulders. Three strands of disk-shaped gold and faience beads were around the neck.

The golden mask weighed about twenty-four pounds. Its inlays covered almost the entire surface. The stripes of the *nemes* headdress and the beard contain colored glass in imitation of lapis lazuli. The eyebrows and inlaid parts around the eye, however, are real lapis lazuli. The whites of the eyes consist of quartz, and the areas of the iris and pupil are obsidian. Since no distinction is made between these two parts, there is no defined pupil, and the eyes never focus on any one point. The collar includes sections of colored glass, turquoise, quartz, and other semiprecious stones.

An inscription equating the elements of the mask with parts of gods covers the shoulders and part of the back of the mask. The facial features of the mask, although similar to those of other representations of Tutankhamun in the tomb, seem to be more lifelike and may represent a portrait of the young king. It was hoped that the myriad steps taken to preserve the king's body would insure a place for him in the Afterlife, so that he might live forever.

BIBLIOGRAPHY

Aldred, C. *Akhenaten and Nefertiti.* London, 1973.

Aldred, C. *Jewels of the Pharaohs.* London, 1971.

Allen, T.G. *The Egyptian Book of the Dead Documents in the Oriental Institute Museum.* Chicago, 1960.

Altenmuller, B. *Synkretismus in den Sargtexten.* Wiesbaden, 1975.

Baker, H.S. *Furniture in the Ancient World.* London, 1966.

Bleeker, C.J. *Habor and Thoth.* Leiden, 1973.

Carter, H. *The Tomb of Tut. Ankh. Amen.* 3 vols. London, 1923-33.

Desroches-Noblecourt, C. *Tutankhamen, Life and Death of a Pharaoh.* London, 1963.

Edwards, I.E.S. *Treasures of Tutankhamun.* New York, 1972.

Edwards, I.E.S., Buckley, T., Wente, E.F. *Treasures of Tutankhamun,* New York, 1976.

Edwards, I.E.S. *Tutankhamun's Jewelry.* New York, 1976.

Faulkner, R. *The Ancient Egyptian Coffin Texts.* Warminster, 1973.

Fox, P. *Tutankhamun's Treasure.* London, 1951.

Harris, J.R. *Lexicographical Studies in Ancient Egyptian Minerals.* Berlin, 1961.

Hayes, W.C. *The Scepter of Egypt. 2 vols. Cambridge, 1959.*

Lange, K. and Hirmer, M. *Egypt-Architecture. Sculpture, Painting.* London, 1968.

Landstrom, B. *Ships of the Pharaohs.* New York, 1970.

Lucas, A. *Ancient Egyptian Materials and Industries.* London, 1962.

Martin, P. *Mummies.* Chicago, 1976.

Morenz, S. *Egyptian Religion.* London, 1973.

Vandier, J. *Manuel d'archeologie egyptienne.* vol. III. Paris, 1958.

Wilkinson, A. *Ancient Egyptian Jewelry.* London, 1971.

Yoyotte, J. *Treasures of the Pharaohs.* Geneva, 1968.